Sand in Their Shoes

Legend has it that once you get the sands of Miami Beach in your shoes, you never get it out; that you are forever affected and destined to return to Miami again and again.

A book about Miami
as conceived by Martin W. Taplin
and written by Sandy Thorpe

With special thanks to

Martin W. Taplin, Esq.
Paul S. George, Ph.D.
George Swartz
and Kathy Sherman

ISBN 0-9764147-0-8
Books In Print

TABLE OF CONTENTS

TABLE OF CONTENTS
(cont'd)

The Magic City

Join us for a leisurely stroll
down Miami's sandy shores and
meet some of the people whose
passage through our city
helped put the Magic in
Miami and Miami on the map.

These are the men and
women who would forever
after always have a
little sand in
their shoes...

Pedro Menendez de Aviles

La Florida
1527 - 1598

South Florida
1898

South Florida
1917

What's in a Name?

Named after Lake Okeechobee which was originally called **"Lake Mayaimi,"** the Indian name for "big water" or "sweet water," **Miami** was first colonized by Spanish **Admiral Pedro Menendez de Aviles**, who established the first European mission on the north bank of the Miami River in 1567.

The area had been discovered more than 50 years previously by another Spanish explorer, **Juan Ponce de Leon**, who sailed into Biscayne Bay in 1513, and marked the place on his map as "Chequescha" - his interpretation of "Tequesta" – for the natives that lived there.

Juan Ponce de Leon

 In 1998, the 38-foot wide "Miami Circle" was discovered in downtown Miami at the mouth of the Miami River. Tequesta in origin, carbon-dating tests have found charcoal fragments from the site to be about 2,000 years old.

 *Biscayne Bay is said to have been named for a former member of the Spanish court who resided on one of the islands in the Bay, **Don Pedro el Biscaino**. "Bischiyano" is also an Indian name meaning "the favorite path of the rising moons."*

Spain controlled Florida for the next 200 years until, in 1763, it was ceded to Britain as part of the Treaty of Paris in order to ransom back Havana which the English had captured.

British ownership of Florida triggered a mass migration from the American colonies. The Creek Indians from Georgia, fleeing southward to escape slavery in the British controlled northern colonies, came to be known in Florida as the "Seminoles," a name which evolved from the term "istî siminolî" in their native "Maskókî" language meaning "free people."

The "Maskókî" dialect, known today as "Mikisúkî," is from whence the modern "Miccosukee" name is derived, and distinguishes those Seminoles who settled south of "Lake Mayaimi" (Lake Okeechobee).

The name "Seminole" also comes from the term "Cimarron(es)" in Spanish, meaning "fugitive," "renegade" or "wild men."

"The Freedom Hero"
Seminole Leader Osceola

 The Miccosukee Tribe of Florida was formed in 1961, independent of the Seminole Tribe of Florida which was formed in 1957.

The most famous of these "wild men renegades" was the Seminole leader **Osceola**. Under his leadership during the Second Seminole War in 1835, the Seminoles slaughtered **Major Francis Langhorn Dade** along with 109 of his soldiers in what is commonly known as the "Dade Massacre" and then, four days later, proceeded to defeat **General Duncan Clinch** and 750 of his men. Dade County, which at that time also included most of today's Broward, Palm Beach and Martin counties, was named for the fallen major the following year.

General Duncan Clinch

Massacre of Major Francis Langhorn Dade

In addition, in their migration southward, the Seminoles brutalized the remaining Tequesta Indians who had not already fallen to European disease. Fearing the Seminoles more than the Spanish, the surviving Tequestas were boatlifted to Havana.

As protection against the Seminole Indians, the U.S. began building Fort Dallas on the banks of the Miami River in 1837.

Then, in one of the blackest marks in American military history, **Osceola** was lured into a trap by **General Thomas Jessup** under a flag of truce. He was arrested and imprisoned in Fort Moultrie near Charleston, where he contracted a fatal illness and died in 1838.

In 1842, **William English** platted the **"Village of Miami"** on the south bank of the Miami River on Fort Dallas land previously owned by his uncle, **Richard Fitzpatrick**. Fitzpatrick had purchased the Bahamian-held lands (known today as Coconut Grove) in 1830, and established a slave plantation, but was forced out by the Seminoles.

In 1844, the County seat was moved from Indian Key to Miami and the 1850 census reported 96 residents living in the area. However, with the Everglades teeming with alligators to the west, and the Atlantic Ocean to the east, expansion was difficult. Add to that the Third Indian War which lasted from 1855 to 1857, and by 1860, only the natives remained and the name **"Miami"** no longer appeared in public records.

General Thomas Jessup

"A rose by any other name would smell as sweet."
                                    - William Shakespeare

The Wreckers

Spanish galleons laden with treasure would pass through Florida's straits beckoning all manner of pirates, scalawags, thieves and wreckers; men who survived off the salvage of ships wrecked against the treacherous coral reef. Several "life saving stations" or "houses of refuge" were established along the coastline to search for these stranded ships; one of the earliest being located in what is now the *Altos del Mar* area of Miami Beach at 77th and Collins Ave.

While Key West offered safe haven to many of these brigands, the early 1800s saw the likes of Tampa's infamous pirate **"Gasparilla" (José Gaspar),** a former officer in the Royal Spanish Navy credited with capturing more than 400 ships, seducing countless women and eventually betraying the King of Spain, and his arch-rival, Miami's own **"Black Caesar,"** the "African Prince-Pirate" **(Henri Caesar),** a Haitian slave of French parentage who is said to have buried millions of dollars in gold, silver and gems in Caesar's Creek (the area between Biscayne Bay and the Atlantic Ocean) and all along Florida's east and west coasts.

Though rivals, some historians believe Caesar and Gasparilla eventually formed a partnership and that both died together in a battle with an American warship. Others claim Caesar was captured by the Navy and burned to death tied to a tree in Key West, the fire being lit by the widow of a preacher whose eyes Caesar had burned out.

So many ships were lost during this period that the U.S. Government built a 65-foot tall lighthouse on Key Biscayne in 1825. Destroyed by Seminoles in 1836, it was rebuilt in 1846, and in 1855, it was raised to 95 feet. Inactive since 1878, the Cape Florida Lighthouse is Dade County's oldest standing structure.

The Pirate "Gasparilla"

"And I hear from the outgoing ship in the bay the song of the sailors in glee ...and wait for the signal to go to the shore, to the ship that is waiting for me."
- Bret Harte

Today, there are more than 40 shipwrecks located within the boundaries of Biscayne National Park, several just off Miami Beach.

The Homesteaders

The climate, the mosquitos and the constant threat of Indian attack made homesteading in South Florida less than desirable. So much so, in fact, that the United States Congress passed the Armed Occupation Act in 1842, offering 160 acres of land to anyone who would settle in the area, build a home, improve the land, and survive for five years. There were few takers.

Four years earlier, in 1838, **Dr. Henry Perrine**, a physician and botanist from Illinois, had been awarded 36 square miles of land in South Dade for the purpose of cultivating a subtropical nursery. Hemp based, his research was partly for the treatment of tropical diseases and was also expected to save the United States millions of dollars each year in the production of rope, twine, burlap and other similar products. Unfortunately, Perrine was killed just two years later in an Indian attack along with six other early homesteaders. His family managed to escape unharmed, but they quickly left the area and the land remained dormant until his son, **Henry Perrine, Jr.** finally exercised the provisions of the grant many years later.

Sarah Anne Perrine Rogers
Henry Perrine, Jr.
Hester Marie Perrine Walker

Ephraim Sturtevant

Originally called "Perrineville", today this area encompasses Kendall, the Village of Pinecrest, Perrine, South Dade, Palmetto Bay and Cutler Ridge, named for **Dr. William C. Cutler**, a wealthy physician from Massachusetts who settled in the area in 1883.

By the latter part of the 1850s, after the Third Indian War, tensions eased and **William** and **Emily Wagner** built a house on the Miami River just west of Fort Dallas, where they sold beverages to the Seminoles. A devout Catholic, modern Catholicism began at **William Wagner's** house, where Miami's first masses were held.

The end of the Civil War brought the "carpetbaggers," including **Ephraim Sturtevant (Julia Tuttle's** father) and **William H. Gleason**, who would amass an incredible 1.35 million acres of land during his tenure as self-appointed Governor of Florida, which he purchased from the government for a mere six cents an acre.

Still, an 1895 census listed only 9 residents living in the area.

"Be it ever so humble, there's no place like home."
- John Howard Payne

Dade County's oldest archeological find was unearthed in the Cutler area, locating fossils and Tequesta artifacts dating back more than 10,000 years.

The Wagner Homestead is Miami's oldest residence that is still standing. Built in 1857, it was moved to its current location in Lummus Park in 1979.

*Today's Seybold Canal was originally named Wagner Creek; named for **William Wagner**.*

The Pioneers

Early Settlers in Coconut Grove
1896 - 1897

Back row (L-R):
    Mrs. Thomas Monroe, Miss Flora McFarlane, Mrs. Kirk Munroe, Edward A. Hine,
    Mrs. Thomas A. Hine.

Middle row (L-R):
    Dr. Tiger, Ralph M. Munroe, Mrs. E. P. Brown, Miss Brown, Charles E. Stowe,
    Thomas A. Hine, Count James L. Nugent, E. P. Brown.

Bottom row (L-R):
    Kirk Munroe, Count Jean D'Hedouville, Alfred Munroe.

Miami's Godfather

In the beginning... there was sand and surf. Then came **Henry Morrison Flagler**, "Miami's Benevolent Dictator."

It was 1878 when **Henry Flagler** made his first visit to Florida. He was 48 years old and already a wealthy retired oil magnate whose former partner was **John D. Rockefeller** and the Standard Oil Company. Over the next 25 years he would transform Florida from a largely uninhabited swampland to a tropical paradise flourishing with hotels, tourists, cities, agriculture and a railroad system that extended from St. Augustine all the way down to Key West.

Henry Morrison Flagler

"A journey of a thousand miles begins with a single step."
- Confucius

Flagler Street was originally Miami's 12th Street. It was renamed in 1920.
*The Flagler Memorial, which still stands on picturesque Flagler Monument Island across from Star Island, was built on land dredged from Biscayne Bay by **Carl Fisher** in 1922.*

The "Mother of Miami"

Someone once said, "behind every great man, there is a woman" and in **Henry Flagler's** case, this was a widow from Cleveland; a visionary named **Julia D. Tuttle**. From the moment Julia first settled on "the most impressive piece of land she had seen" on the banks of the Miami River in 1891, she beseeched Flagler to extend his railroad to Miami, but he wasn't interested.

Julia D. Tuttle

 *Tragically, **Julia Tuttle** died from a sudden illness in 1898. She was only 48 years old. The Julia Tuttle Causeway (US 195) was built in 1961.*

James E. Ingraham

Henry B. Plant

Undeterred, Julia enlisted the support of another railroad man she had befriended in Ohio, **James E. Ingraham,** a railroad engineer who was president of both **Henry S. Sanford's** intrastate South Florida Railroad Company and **Henry B. Plant's** Southern Railroad which connected north Florida to the southwest coast.

With all good intentions, Ingraham embarked on an expedition to lay tracks across the Everglades, a seemingly insurmountable task, but got lost en route. Fortunately, he was rescued by an Indian who then delivered him to Julia Tuttle's. Still, there was no railroad in Miami.

The winter of 1894-1895 brought a devastating frost to the South which destroyed all of Central Florida's citrus crops as far south as Palm Beach.

In a shrewd move, it is said that Julia Tuttle took advantage of the situation by sending Ingraham (who was now trustee for **Henry Flagler's** East Coast Railway) to deliver a Miami-grown orange blossom along with photographs of the region to Flagler, proving that South Florida was untouched by the frost. Intrigued, Flagler came down to the area to check things out for himself and before the day was out, Tuttle had convinced him to bring his railroad to Miami.

The infant city of Miami didn't develop slowly like other cities; "it arrived in a railroad car, howling and kicking its way into life."

It is the only U.S. city to have been planned by a woman.

> *"No man succeeds without a good woman behind him."*
> **- Harold MacMillan**

*Accused of having an affair with **Julia Tuttle**, a white woman, the Indian that rescued Ingraham had his ear cut off and was banished from his Seminole tribe.*

The "Father of Fort Lauderdale"

At the same time the "Mother of Miami" was seeing her dream of making Miami the "Gateway to the Americas" become a reality, **Frank Stranahan**, a steel worker and steamboat captain (who was also from Ohio) was earning the title of "Father of Fort Lauderdale."

Frank Stranahan

*The Stranahan House, which is located at 335 SE 6th Ave. on the New River, was built by **Frank Stranahan** for his wife **Ivy,** in 1901. The New River is the deepest river in the United States for its length.*

Stranahan's cousin, stagecoach driver **Guy Metcalf**, had established a camp on the New River. When Stranahan came down to assume management of the overland mail route from Lantana to Coconut Grove in 1893, he rebuilt the New River Camp, renamed it "Stranahan House," and turned it into a hotel and frontier trading post. (He also operated the area's first ferry, became its first postmaster and opened its first bank.)

Guy Metcalf

The trading post, which was a South Florida landmark by 1895, gave birth to what would become Fort Lauderdale, named for **Major William Lauderdale**, a Tennessee Volunteer who had fought in the Second Seminole War.

When **Henry Flagler's** railroad rolled through in 1896, it ended Stranahan's ferry business. Thirty years later, losses he sustained in the 1926 hurricane coupled with a declining stock market proved too much for him. Dogged by creditors, "The Father of Fort Lauderdale" committed suicide by jumping in the New River on May 22, 1929.

"Successes have many fathers, failures have none."
- Philip Caldwell

Actually, there were three Fort Lauderdales; the first at the fork of New River; the second at Tarpon Bend; and the largest on the beach at the site of today's Bahia Mar. Fort Lauderdale was incorporated as a town on March 27, 1911, and as a city in 1915.

of traumas during its first
troyed much of the
morning after
ess, trouble-
t troops
men
Miami
erican
the
om-
ear
pi-
lies
eek
ing
l.

early
d by
v cen-
ntained
and agri-
ief econom-
neighborhoods
f the river. Miami
iance for that of a small

reverish real estate industry for
east Florida as large
lions of acres of r
of Florida, th
in many p
vory sal
sold u
was u
an e
ket

By
ha
w
ar
m
Str
had
Mia
ough
for th
establisl
cachet co
opening of
store's new five-
"skyscraper," in 191

William Barnwell Brickell

*Prior to construction of the first bridge across the Miami River, **William Brickell** ran a ferry
service providing passage across the river.*

The Real Deal

Real ESTATE, that is.

William and **Mary Brickell** and their large family arrived in Miami at the outset of the 1870s and purchased land in the settlement of Fort Lauderdale as well as hundreds of acres on the south side of the Miami River where Fort Dallas once stood. Since they owned the property directly across from **Julia Tuttle**, **Henry Flagler** agreed to a deal that would extend his railway from Palm Beach to Miami in exchange for their combined hundreds of acres of prime real estate.

In another shrewd move, Julia sold Flagler only half of her 620 acres on the River, retaining every other lot for herself. Flagler also had to agree to build a hotel at the end of the route at the mouth of the Miami River and to supply water and electricity to the area in order to seal the deal.

The deal was struck and Flagler was now ready to lay the foundation for a city on both sides of the Miami River.

The City of Miami was incorporated on July 28, 1896, three months after Flagler's railroad arrived.

"The best investment on Earth, is earth."
- **Louis J. Glickman**

 Brickell Avenue was once strictly residential and home to the "Robber Barons" of the Industrial Revolution. Today, Brickell Avenue remains the backbone of the city's financial community and is home to more than 70 international banks and hundreds of local, national and international corporations. Formerly known as "Millionaire's Row", luxurious multi-million dollar residences dotted the Avenue with breathtaking views of Biscayne Bay.

Cocoanut Grove

Two decades before there was a "Miami," there was a thriving community of mostly Bahamian seamen located in the hammocks on the edge of Biscayne Bay. Originally called "Jack's Bight" in honor of **"Jolly Jack" Peacock**, one of the area's first settlers, today this lush tropical village is known as Coconut Grove, or "The Grove" for short.

Several important pioneers resided in this area in the 1880s and '90s, including Jack's brother **Charles**, and Charles' wife **Isabella**. Prompted by a charismatic **Ralph Munroe**, a yacht designer from New York who was friends with **William** and **Mary Brickell**, the Peacocks built the area's very first hotel, the Bay View House.

Charles Peacock

Isabella Peacock

Today's beautiful Peacock Park occupies the location where the Bay View House (renamed the Peacock Inn) once stood.

Ralph Middleton Munroe

 Built in 1891, **Ralph Munroe's** house (The Barnacle) is located at 3485 Main Highway in Coconut Grove. (Public)

Soon thereafter, Munroe enticed his wealthy northern friends down to the area, including plant explorers **Robert H. Montgomery** and **David Fairchild** (who was married to **Alexander Graham Bell's** daughter), and the Bay View House, renamed the Peacock Inn, thrived.

Thrilled with **Ralph Munroe's** contribution, the Peacocks sold Munroe 40 acres of their bayfront land for $400 and one of his sailboats. Partly built from salvaged ship timber, his residence, which he named "The Barnacle," is Dade County's oldest home that has remained in its original location. Surviving both the 1926 hurricane and Hurricane Andrew in 1992, it is now a state historical site and tourist attraction.

David Grandison Fairchild

Robert H. Montgomery

Dr. David Fairchild's residence, which he called "The Kampong" is located on 10 acres at 4013 Douglas Road in Coconut Grove. A frequent visitor to the Kampong, Alexander Graham Bell invented a method of obtaining palatable drinking water from sea water with an apparatus that utilized solar power. The device still remains at the property. (Private)

Other important settlers of the time were **Charles E. Stowe,** who was one of the area's first preachers, **Flora McFarlane,** who became Coconut Grove's first schoolteacher, and **James William Ewan,** a New Jersey migrant who succeeded **William H. Gleason** in the State Legislature. Gleason, a Reconstruction "carpetbagger," had been known in political circles as the "King of Dade." To distinguish him from his predecessor, the flamboyant Ewan was labeled the "Duke of Dade," a title that reflected his position, proper dress, mannerisms and social graces. Friend to the Brickells, some said Ewan may have also been romantically involved with **Julia Tuttle.**

James W. Ewan

Miss Flora McFarlane

Charles E. Stowe was the son of author Harriet Beecher Stowe who wrote "Uncle Tom's Cabin." The McFarlane Homestead Historic District (roughly bordered by Jefferson St., Frow Ave., Brooker St. and Grand Avenue), as well as McFarlane Street in The Grove were named after this important pioneer.

At the same time, noted author of books for boys **Kirk Munroe** (no relation to Ralph) and his wife **Mary Barr Munroe** built a house in the area. One of Florida's earliest conservationists, in an effort to save the egrets from poachers, Mrs. Munroe founded the Southern Tropical Audubon Society.

Mary was also the first president of the Dade County Federation of Women's Clubs and formed a literary group called the Pine Needle Club. As a visitor, **Mrs. Andrew Carnegie** was so impressed with Mrs. Munroe's work, that she sent her a supply of books - and the Coconut Grove Library was born, of which husband Kirk became librarian.

It was at this time that **Mary Barr Munroe**, at the insistence of **David Fairchild**, made the decision to drop the "a" from "Cocoanut" Grove, even though book plates had already been made with the "a" included.

Mary Barr Munroe

*According to **Ralph Munroe**, naming the town Coconut Grove was pure coincidence. "The coconuts were planted afterwards so that the town could live up to its name."*

In 1887, **Ralph** and **Kirk Munroe**, along with several other residents, founded the Biscayne Bay Yacht Club. Ralph was elected "Commodore," a title that he held for 22 years, and Kirk became its secretary, a position he held for 35 years. The Biscayne Bay Yacht Club still exists at the foot of Main Street in The Grove and is the oldest organization in Miami-Dade County.

In 1893, **Kirk Munroe** was voted "most popular author" by more than 10,000 youngsters at the Chicago World's Fair. During his lifetime, Kirk would eventually write 37 books and numerous magazine and newspaper articles. The Library of Congress has "Archival Manuscript Material;" the papers of **Kirk Munroe**, consisting of more than 2,500 items.

In addition, **Ralph Munroe** brought a camera with him to Coconut Grove in 1883, and over the next 32 years would take a series of 727 photographs from dry-plate negatives that depicted the people, places and daily activities in the area he called home. He also wrote numerous articles and a book, "The Commodore's Story," which was published in 1930.

These writings and photographs remain some of South Florida's greatest historical treasures.

Kirk Munroe

"Where your treasure is, there will your heart be also."
- Matthew vi.21.

It Was a Very Good Year

1896 – With 344 votes, Miami is incorporated as a city, and **John B. Reilly**, an Irish-Catholic, is elected the city's first Mayor.

The first registered voter was **Silos Austin**, a black man.

John B. Reilly

 *Although its citizens wanted to honor the man responsible for the city's development by naming it "Flagler," **Henry Flagler** declined the honor in favor of keeping the old Indian name "Miami." The name "Fort Dallas" was also under consideration.*

Other 1896 settlers were:

Jack Graham, Miami's first City Clerk;

J.A. McDonald, who was in charge of Flagler System construction in Miami;

Frank T. Budge, who opened a hardware store;

J.A. McDonald

Frank T. Budge

William Mack Brown, who opened the first bank, the Bank of Bay Biscayne;

Dr. James M. Jackson, a physician for **Henry Flagler's** railroad and later Miami, in whose memory Jackson Memorial Hospital is named;

Dr. James M. Jackson

*Jackson Memorial Hospital was originally named the Miami City Hospital. It was renamed in Jackson's honor after his death in 1924. **John Sewell's** house, "Halissee Hall," still stands on the complex. Located at 190 S.E. 12th Terrace in Miami, the office and surgery of **Dr. James M. Jackson** was built in 1905, and is now home to the Dade Heritage Trust. (Private)*

Isidor Cohen, Miami's first Jewish merchant who sponsored the city's first Jewish congregation, Congregation Beth David, and his wife **Ida**, founder of Miami's Jewish Home for the Aged;

Isidor Cohen

Ida Cohen

Founded in 1912, the Beth David Congregation is now located at 2625 S.W. 3rd Avenue in Miami, where it moved to in 1949. The Miami Jewish Home for the Aged opened in December 1945, and today is housed on the 7-acre wooded estate of Douglas Gardens, 5200 N.E. 2nd Ave.

John Seybold, a journeyman baker for whom Miami's Seybold Building is named;

John Seybold

 The 10-story Seybold Building, located at 36 N.E. Flagler Street, is the world's largest jewelry center housing more than 300 stores and $1 billion of jewelry on the premises.

"Big John" and **Everest G. Sewell**, brothers who would become two of Miami's most admired leaders, both serving as mayor; the latter being elected three times; and

"Ev" and "Big John" Sewell

J.E. Lummus, who opened a general store and then, 16 years later, along with his brother **John**, partnered with **John Collins** and **Carl Fisher** to build a bridge that connected the mainland to what would become Miami Beach.

J.E. Lummus, John Sewell, T.L. Townley, E.G. Sewell

"Make no little plans; they have no magic to stir men's blood...
Make big plans; aim high in hope and work."
- Daniel Burnham

 J.E. Lummus was the second Mayor of Miami; J.N. was the first Mayor of Miami Beach.

Money Talks

As **Henry Flagler** extended his Florida East Coast Railway southward, he strategically built hotels and resorts along the route. He kept his promise to **Julia Tuttle** and, just three weeks after the devastating Christmas fire of 1896 destroyed most of Miami's business district, Flagler opened his magnificent 5-story, 400+-room Royal Palm Hotel at the "end-of-the-line" in Miami. **Jacob Astor** and his family were the hotel's first guests.

Wealthy northern industrialists, America's "Guilded Age Princes," flocked to Miami and started the soon-to-be-famous Miami winter season. Frequent visitors included Chicagoan **James Deering**, a manufacturer of farming equipment (International Harvester) who later built Villa Vizcaya, former Secretary of State **William Jennings Bryan, Louis Comfort Tiffany, Andrew Carnegie, John D. Rockefeller** and the **Vanderbilt** family.

James Deering
International Harvester Company

John D. Rockefeller
Standard Oil Company

Andrew Carnegie
Mellon Bank, N.A.

Louis Comfort Tiffany
Tiffany's Jewelers

Bryan, Tiffany and **William H. Luden** of cough drop fame were among those who built winter homes in the area, as did **Joe and Jennie Weiss**, restaurateurs whose famous "Joe's Stone Crab" is still a Miami Beach landmark.

Joe and Jennie Weiss

 Joe's Stone Crab is located at 11 Washington Avenue in Miami Beach and is still family owned. It is open during Stone Crab Season only, October 15 through May 15.

With the new century came a new newspaper, the *Miami Evening Record*, forerunner of the *Miami Herald*. Its editor-in-chief was Judge **Frank B. Stoneman**, father of Florida's "Defender of the Everglades," **Marjory Stoneman Douglas**.

Having built Flagler's Royal Palm Hotel with his brother John, **Everest G. Sewell** was now a wealthy merchant and began heavily promoting the city.

Miami was no longer a small southern town.

Frank B. Stoneman (on porch) with Marjory (in arms)
1893

"Wealth is the product of a man's capacity to think."
- Ayn Rand

The "Miami Evening Record," renamed the "News Record," became the "Miami Herald" when
Frank B. Shutts *took control of the paper in 1910.*

Giant Steps

Thomas J. Pancoast
Leads the Way at the
Opening of Collins' Bridge
Connecting Miami to Miami Beach
June 12, 1913

Getting Connected

How low can you go? For **Henry Flagler**, Miami wasn't far enough, so, in 1904, he began the incredible task of extending his FEC Railway "over the sea," connecting Miami's mainland to Key West.

So improbable a feat, and considering Flagler's advancing years and declining health, many believed it could not be done and what would be his last venture was often referred to as "Flagler's Folly."

But, with the help of chief construction engineer **William J. Krome** (for whom Krome Avenue was named) and bridge-building expert **Clarence S. Coe** – plus $27 million of Flagler's own money – and despite Mother Nature plaguing his efforts with five separate hurricanes, three of them severe, causing devastating damages and costing hundreds of lives, on January 22, 1912, a frail 82-year old **Henry Flagler** rode into Key West on his private railcar.

No longer "Flagler's Folly," this engineering marvel was now hailed as the "Eighth Wonder of the World," second only in importance to the construction of the Panama Canal.

William J. Krome

John S. Collins

At the same time Flagler's railroad was connecting St. Augustine to Miami and then Key West, **Dr. John Wescott** and **George L. Bradley**, along with $100,000 invested by **Henry Flagler**, connected the St. John's River near Jacksonville to Biscayne Bay by what is now called the Intracoastal Waterway. Originally conceived to be a significant player in shipping fruits and vegetables, the waterway was not completed until 1912, and by then Flagler's railroad had cornered the market on transportation to the north.

Too narrow and shallow for ships large enough to carry substantial cargo, it served no purpose for men like horticulturist **John Collins**.

Considered to be a pioneer in the area of fruit development, Collins looked to the barrier strip immediately east of Flagler's new city, determined to grow something that wasn't already plentiful. He decided on avocados and planted 2,945 avocado trees on the west side of Indian Creek. The original pine trees he planted as a windbreak still line today's Pine Tree Drive at 41st Street.

With only a ferry service as transportation between the mainland and the newly developing Miami Beach, Collins found the process of transporting his crops to Flagler's railroad a tedious process. So, in 1911, he decided to build a canal from Indian Creek to Biscayne Bay.

Already an old man and low on cash, Collins turned to his children for help. Sons **Lester, Arthur** and **Irving Collins**, Irving's wife, and son-in-law **Thomas Pancoast** and his wife **Katherine**, came down to Florida to assess the situation for themselves. Seeing the potential for real estate development as well as its agricultural benefits, they agreed to give Collins the money for his canal — if he also agreed to build a bridge across the bay.

After getting permission from the U.S. War Department, Collins' bridge, "the longest wooden bridge in the world," opened on June 12, 1913.

> *"Don't be afraid to take a big step. You can't cross a chasm in two small jumps."*
> **- David Lloyd George**

In 1913, the Collins family deeded their oceanfront property between 21st and 22nd Streets to the City of Miami as a permanent "public park and recreation ground." This area, in the heart of today's Art Deco District, is known as Collins Park. World-famous Collins Avenue (originally named Atlantic Boulevard) was renamed in Collins' honor in 1914.

Build It and They Will Come

John Collins and **Thomas Pancoast** formed the Miami Beach Improvement Company and, as the bridge and canal were being completed, built hotels and casinos along the way.

Thomas J. Pancoast

 At the time, casinos were buildings that were used for entertainment and dancing, and not necessarily gambling.

Then, in 1913, they hired the "type of salesman who could make a good living selling ice to the Eskimos," **Edward "Doc" Dammers**, who would auction off 100 of their lots in a frantic 4-day only sale. The pace was set when 104 lots were sold; four more than were supposed to be.

Edward "Doc" Dammers

At the same time, **James E.** and **John N. Lummus** (who preferred to use their initials rather than their first names) owned 580 acres of land on the southern end of the beach (today's South Beach). Both local bankers, they were the ones who loaned Collins the money to start his bridge. The brothers formed the Ocean Beach Realty Company and built small vacation homes.

J.E. Lummus

J.N. Lummus

 *In 1915, **J.N.** Lummus sold the land from 5th to 15th Streets at Ocean Drive to the City for $40,000, stipulating that it be used for a park in perpetuity (Lummus Park). Several years later, when he was bankrupt, Lummus asked the City of Miami Beach for reversionary rights so the park could be sold for commercial purposes, but the city council turned him down.*

Across the Bay, **Charles Deering,** CEO of International Harvester, had purchased 368 acres in the Cutler area and his half-brother **James Deering** was employing 10% of Miami's population building Villa Vizcaya.

Charles Deering

The 360-acre **Charles Deering** Estate is located at SW 167th St. and Old Cutler Rd. on what is arguably the choicest piece of real estate in Dade County. Today, the Estate is managed by the Miami-Dade Park & Recreation Department in conjunction with the Deering Estate Foundation. (Public)

James Deering's 70-room Villa Vizcaya, located at 3251 S. Miami Avenue in Miami is now a museum. (Public)

Simultaneously, Bayfront Park was created by more dredging under the supervision of merchant **E.G. Sewell** who was busy promoting the city of Miami and conducting Miami's very first campaign to lure, not land owners, but vacationers – the tourists.

It was Sewell who was responsible for bringing the first airplane to Miami and convincing famed aviator **Glenn Curtiss** to open a flying school at what is today's Dinner Key. It was at this school that Curtiss trained our dogfighting Marine Pilots in World War I.

Everest G. Sewell

 E.G. Sewell *was responsible for bringing the first Royal Poinciana trees to the area.*

Seeing the value of the real estate in South Florida, Curtiss and fellow investor Missouri cattleman **James Bright**, developed and built the city of Hialeah, the "Gateway to the Everglades," and Curtiss became its first mayor.

Land sold so quickly in Hialeah that Curtiss went on to design and build the Moorish-themed city of Opa-Locka, and Bright went on to build Miami Springs, originally called "Country Club Estates."

Curtiss was also responsible for bringing the game of Jai Alai to Miami in 1924. An immediate success, Jai Alai became one of Miami's largest annual tourist attractions.

Glenn Curtiss

 The original Seminole name for Opa-Locka was Opatishawocka-Locka which, loosely translated, means "Big Swamp."

This was the climate that **Carl Fisher**, aka "Mr. Miami Beach," came into when he got sand in his shoes and started acquiring land on the beach in exchange for loans, some of which he made to the Lummus brothers.

Born in 1874, **Carl Graham Fisher** was a self-made millionaire by the age of 35. He then went on to build the Indianapolis Motor Speedway (host to the "Indianapolis 500" touted as "the greatest spectacle in sports"); the Lincoln Highway (now Route 30), which was our nation's first cross-country road connecting New York to San Francisco; and the Dixie Highway, which originated from his home state of Indiana and ran through the Deep South — all the way down to Fisher's paradise — Miami Beach.

Carl Graham Fisher

It was **Carl Fisher** who loaned Collins the $50,000 he needed to *complete* his bridge - which Fisher did in exchange for 200 acres of Collins' land on the beach.

Once Fisher realized that sand could hold up a real estate sign, he began a campaign to attract wealthy northerners to purchase his land. Then, in 1924, Florida changed the state constitution to prohibit income and inheritance taxes, making Miami and the beaches even more alluring to the rich.

The Lummus brothers had a different approach. Their vacation homes were of more modest means and they welcomed anyone who was "white, law-abiding, and could afford the property payments."

The population swelled.

Miami Beach was incorporated in 1915, and elected **J.N. Lummus** its first mayor, followed by **Thomas Pancoast**. Over the next decade, by a series of aggressive, and often bizarre, advertising and marketing "gimmicks" — plus massive dredging of sand from Biscayne Bay — Collins, Pancoast, Fisher and Lummus would transform Miami Beach into "America's Winter Playground."

 *While the Lummus brothers sold the City Lummus Park on the ocean in South Beach, stipulating it for permanent public use, and **John Collins** donated land for Collins Park on the ocean between 21st and 23rd, **Carl Fisher** wanted to reserve his prime oceanfront sites for the homes of the wealthy. Despite the significance of his contribution to the area, practically the only memorial to his promotional genius is a monument in Fisher Park on Alton Road in Miami Beach with a bust and a plaque that reads, "He carved a great city out of a jungle." He most surely did.*

1915 also saw the formation of Broward County, named for **Napoleon Bonaparte Broward** who was Florida's 19th governor, serving from 1905 to 1909.

In 1918, sewing machine heir **Paris Singer** commissioned **Addison Mizner** to build a resort that was bigger, better and more ostentatious than any of **Henry Flagler's** hotels. The bizarre architect, who often carried a spider monkey on his shoulder wherever he went, was given full creative license, with the only stipulation being that it be painted anything but Flagler's trademark yellow and white. Money was no object.

The resultant "Bastard-Spanish-Moorish-Romanesque-Gothic-Renaissance-Bull-Market-Damn-the-Expense Style" inspired the imagination of builders all over the state. Mizner became the darling of Palm Beach society and built more than 30 residences, clubs (including the Everglades Club), hotels, shops and churches in the area that is now Boca Raton.

Addison Mizner

 *The **Stephen Sondheim** and **John Weidman** musical, "Gold" (formerly named "Wise Guys") includes some musical numbers written by **Irving Berlin** and centers around the lives of **Addison Mizner** and his equally bizarre brother, **Wilson**, who was a reported dope-addict, gambler and con-artist.*

Back towards the city, **George Edgar Merrick** was building the beautiful city of Coral Gables. To market his planned community, he enlisted famed politician and orator **William Jennings Bryan** who promoted the city as "America's Most Beautiful Suburb" with its modern Mediterranean style, Venetian fountains and Spanish-named boulevards — and hired the flamboyant **Edward E. "Doc" Dammers** of Miami Beach fame to sell lots in frenzied auctions held off the back of a wagon. "Doc" became Coral Gables' first mayor and Merrick, who had always had a great love for Florida and its history, was elected to serve as the Historical Association of Southern Florida's first president.

George Edgar Merrick

William Jennings Bryan

N.B.T. Roney

*The "Village of Merrick Park," one of South Florida's ritziest shopping malls located off U.S. 1 in Coral Gables, was named in **George Merrick's** honor.*

North of Miami, entrepreneur **Joseph Wesley Young** was following in **George Merrick's** footsteps. Adopting Merrick's "City Beautiful" concept, he designed and built his "Dream City" of Hollywood, Florida.

With its extensive coastline, Spanish and Moorish architecture, tropical parks, and broad landscaped boulevards lined with stately rows of palm trees, Hollywood, which was originally named "Hollywood-By-the-Sea," was incorporated in 1925.

Joseph Wesley Young

 Part of Young's original city plan, Hollywood's three trademark traffic circles, Young Circle, Watson Circle and Presidential Circle, were originally named Harding Circle, City Hall Circle and Academy Circle, respectively. Young was also responsible for the development of what would become one of the busiest seaports in Florida, Port Everglades.

Meanwhile, the Georgia-born **Tatum Brothers, J.H., Smiley, B.B. and J.R.,** owned and developed land that extended as far north as today's Surfside, Bal Harbour and Bay Harbor Islands and as far west as the Everglades; 200,000 acres of which they developed for agriculture and habitation. They also built the beautiful communities of Riverside, Riverside Heights and Grove Park west of downtown Miami, as well as Florida City in South Dade. Aggressive marketers, their beachfront *Altos Del Mar* property completely sold out in a single morning and is still considered some of the choicest real estate in Miami Beach today.

Front Row Center: Governor and Mrs. Cary A. Hardee
Far Left: Everest G. Sewell
Back Row Center: Mr. & Mrs. Bethel B. Tatum
with daughter Mrs. Frank H. Fleer

The Tatums also started the first trolley service in Miami, although it was discontinued after only one year of operation.

At the same time, efforts were being made (and dollars were being spent) by millionaire **Barron G. Collier** to complete a highway begun in 1915 by realtor **James F. Jaudon**. This "most amazing highway" connected South Florida's east and west coasts and became known as "The Tamiami Trail," combining the names Tampa and Miami. Collier County was named for the benefactor in 1923.

Barron G. Collier

By 1920, Miami already claimed 30,000 residents and new subdivisions sprang up overnight. From one winter season to the next, the city changed so rapidly that visitors said it had "grown like magic" and Miami came to be known as the "Magic City," a name first coined by newspaperman **E.V. Blackman** back in 1896. Interestingly, Blackman, who was a publicist for Flagler's East Coast Railway in Palm Beach, actually never set foot in Miami.

J.F. Chaille

It was at this time that the City Council, in its infinite wisdom, adopted a plan by Councilman **J.F. Chaille** which divided the city into four quadrants, Northeast, Northwest, Southeast and Southwest, effectively changing the name of every street in Miami (except 6th Street).

12th Street became Flagler Street, dividing the city north and south, and the principal business thoroughfare of Avenue D became Miami Avenue, dividing the city east and west. Such confusing names as " Northwest South River Drive" and "Northwest North River Drive" were the result.

It is said that the mail carriers never recovered.

In 1925, more than 1,000 subdivisions were under construction; Coral Gables, Miami Shores, Lemon City and Coconut Grove all became part of Greater Miami; and the city's population topped 100,000.

Today's
Flagler St. &
Miami Ave.

Miami Street Map
1919

Visitors in the early '20s included **Warren G. Harding**, **Herbert Hoover** and **Franklin D. Roosevelt**; sports heroes like **Knute Rockne** and **Jack Dempsey**; and the next generation of the rich and famous; the **William Kassam Vanderbilt IIs**, the **Astors**, and **C.W. Barron**, founder of the *Wall Street Journal*.

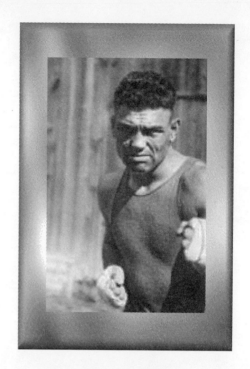

Jack Dempsey

Knute Rockne

Clarence W. Barron

John LaGorce

John Oliver LaGorce, associate editor of *National Geographic Magazine* and a member of the National Geographic Society for 52 years, also came to Miami Beach during this period. Good friends with **Carl Fisher**, LaGorce promoted Miami Beach in his magazine, spotlighting Fisher's own Alton Beach property which he called "Altonia."

In exchange, Fisher provided LaGorce with free automobiles and accommodations, and even named his private Miami Beach golf course in LaGorce's honor.

Carl Fisher

 The LaGorce Country Club is located at 5685 Alton Road in Miami Beach. (Private)

Although **John LaGorce** was a notorious bigot who "did not like women, blacks or Jews – though not necessarily in that order," he cherished the environment and was one of the Everglades' earliest crusaders. In 1928, along with landscape architect **Ernest F. Coe**, **Stephen T. Mather** of the National Park Service, *Miami Herald* reporter **Marjory Stoneman Douglas**, botanist **David Fairchild**, and Congresswoman **Ruth Bryan Owen**, daughter of **William Jennings Bryan**, they formed the Tropic Everglades Park Association and petitioned to gain local support for a national park. **President Harry Truman** would make their dream a reality in 1947.

Marjory Stoneman Douglas

Ruth Bryan Owen

Stephen Tyng Mather

Ernest F. Coe
The "Father of the Everglades"

 Ruth Bryan Owen was named minister to Denmark by President Roosevelt; the first woman in the United States to represent our country overseas. She was elected to Congress twice.

Extravagance was the name of the game and **Carl Fisher** made one of the most extravagant trades in history when he traded his 216-acre tropical island (which he had originally purchased from **D.A. Dorsey**, an early developer of Overtown and Miami's first black millionaire) for **William Vanderbilt's** 220-foot yacht and crew. The Vanderbilts made the island their winter residence and named it "Fisher Island," for their friend. Their mansion still stands and is now the Fisher Island Club and Marina.

William K. Vanderbilt & Wife, Rosamund

The beachfront location and perfect weather combined with rising hemlines, falling morals, lavish spending and the ostentatious lifestyles typical of the Roaring '20s, had Miami and Miami Beach booming. However, speculation drove real estate prices to unsustainable heights and speculators began defaulting on their payments. The national news media reported that all was not well in paradise and that investing in Florida real estate was "risky."

The boom was about to go bust.

"Progress lies not in enhancing what is, but in advancing toward what will be."
- Kahlil Gibran, "A Handful of Sand on the Shore"

 *Fisher Island has been home to some of the world's most famous celebrities, including media mogul **Oprah Winfrey**, screen legend **Anne Bancroft** and funnyman **Mel Brooks**.*

It Was a Very Bad Year

The bubble burst in **1926**. Crime had ascended to an all-time high, the rate of violent deaths soared, and the bootlegging and smuggling industries thrived. Bootleggers obtained liquor from the nearby Bahama Islands and Miami seemed oblivious to Prohibition and its enforcement.

With national inflation on the rise and increasing negative media, wary speculators backed off from further investment, and a series of setbacks brought construction to a standstill.

Flagler's railroad had been shut down since the fall of the previous year for much needed repairs, forcing all building materials to be shipped on the water. Then, early in the year, two large freighters capsized in Miami's harbor, effectively shutting off all incoming or outgoing shipments for several weeks. Once the channel was finally cleared, Miami experienced a mass exodus of speculators.

The delays in building supplies caused many projects to fail, including **N.B.T. Roney's** dream of a Spanish-themed, Bohemian-style artist colony.

Then, on September 17, 1926, a deadly 130 mph hurricane slammed into the city killing hundreds of people and injuring thousands more. Countless homes were destroyed and entire subdivisions flattened. Unable to get building materials, the **Combs** family, undertakers who established Miami's first cemetery, buried the dead in coffins manufactured out of hurricane debris. A devastating depression followed and Miami plunged into the Great Depression three years before the rest of the nation.

Walter Jr. and Walter Sr. Combs

1926 also brought the birth of a man whose power and influence would shape Miami's future for generations to come, **Fidel Castro**.

"In great attempts it is glorious even to fail."
- Vince Lombardi

 *1926 was especially bad for **Carl Fisher**. His wife, **Jane**, divorced him after 17 years of marriage. When they married in 1909, Fisher was 35; Jane was 15.*

Shattered Dreams & New Beginnings

The 1926 Hurricane left more than 17,000 people homeless and shattered a myriad of dreams. Buildings were left unfinished, banks failed, and miles of sidewalks and roads that "went nowhere" were empty.

Flagler's Royal Palm Hotel remained closed that winter season and was demolished within the next few years.

Boca Raton's **Addison Mizner** was bankrupt, as was Hollywood's **Joe Young**.

Where, in 1924, **Carl Fisher** was worth an estimated $50,000,000 - $100,000,000, now he was personally financing the "Miami of the North" – the failed northeastern resort town of Montauk. It proved to be his Waterloo and he began selling off his assets for much needed cash. World War I flying ace and former racecar driver **Eddie Rickenbacker** bought the Indianapolis Speedway from him in 1927.

Edward Vernon Rickenbacker

Despite it all, Miami managed to retain 125,000 residents and kept right on building.

One person who survived the 1926 storm by taking cover in the Seybold Arcade was a 24-year-old police reporter for the *Miami Herald*, **Henry Reno**. Henry would later father future United States Attorney General **Janet Reno**, who was born in 1938.

1927 saw the arrival of a second railroad, the Seaboard Air Line Railroad, owned by **S. Davies Warfield**, whose niece, **Wallis Warfield Simpson**, changed the hierarchy of the British Empire when **King Edward VIII** abdicated the throne of England to marry the woman he loved.

Edward and **Wallis Simpson** became the Duke and Duchess of Windsor.

S. Davies Warfield
(2nd from Left)

Chalk's Flying Service, consisting largely of seaplanes used for rum-running during the Prohibition, built a terminal on the newly created Watson Island, named for early pioneer and three-time Mayor of Miami, **John Watson**. Then, in 1928, Pan American Airways moved to Miami from Key West.

The aviation industry proved to be a driving force in Miami's economic recovery and, that same year, **Harold Pitcairn** hired **Eddie Rickenbacker** to help run *his* newly acquired airline, Pitcairn Airways.

On December 1, 1928, Pitcairn Airways began the first air mail service between Miami and Jacksonville. Previously, mail had been delivered by rail, and before that, because no roads cut all the way through, on foot.

From 1885-1893, South Florida's famous "Barefoot Mailmen" made the 136-mile round-trip journey (80 by foot and 56 by water) from Lake Worth to Fort Dallas on the Miami River and back, in six days.

Harold Pitcairn

Pitcairn Airways was renamed *Eastern* two years later and began the first passenger service to destinations north.

 *In 1931, **John Watson, Jr.** installed the first parking meters in Miami.*

 *Today's Highway A1A follows the route taken by the Barefoot Mailmen. Several memorials are located along this path. A bronze plaque beneath the Hillsboro Lighthouse honors the most famous of these Barefoot Mailmen, **James "Ed" Hamilton**, who died, probably eaten by alligators, while en route to Fort Dallas in 1887.*

Another bright spot was the opening of the largest private university in the South, the University of Miami, which was started by **George Merrick** less than one month after the devastating hurricane. Classes had to be held in a half-completed apartment-hotel instead of its own building which had been destroyed in the storm, but that was typical of Miamians who could not be kept down. On October 23, 1926, the all-freshman football team, aptly named the "Hurricanes" and sporting their familiar "burnt orange, Biscayne green and white" uniforms, won their very first game. On November 3rd, **Dr. Bowman F. Ashe** was elected president and over the next 26 years guided the University through bankruptcy, reorganization and a world war.

Dr. Bowman F. Ashe

1928 brought another element to the city when **Al "Scarface" Capone** settled on Palm Island, a spot he picked so he could easily smuggle in contraband on the water, which was then immediately transferred to waiting trucks hidden in the underbrush for transport and distribution. It was from his Florida home that he orchestrated the fateful St. Valentine's Day Massacre, which took place on February 14, 1929. By the time he was convicted of income tax evasion in 1931, Miami's gambling and alcohol trades had been completely taken over by organized crime.

October 1929 brought the Stock Market Crash and, once again, dreams were shattered and fortunes lost as the nation headed into the Great Depression.

Alphonse "Scarface" Capone

"Our greatest glory is not in never falling, but in rising every time we fall."
- Confucius

Miami on the "Moove"

Many of today's thriving South Florida communities were once prairie land. The name, "Hialeah," for instance, is an Indian name meaning "pretty prairie area," and before **Glenn Curtiss** and **James Bright** developed it, Hialeah was dairy land, Bright having been attracted to the site because he was a cattleman (Curtiss-Bright Dairies).

James Bright

 Ponce de Leon brought the first cows to Florida in 1521; Andalusia cattle, relatives of the Texas longhorn.

So, too, history records as early as 1897, pioneer and founder of South Miami, **W.A. Larkins**, established a small dairy at the southernmost end of the wagon trail that is now the Ingraham Highway (named for **James Ingraham**, trustee for **Henry Flagler's** Florida East Coast Railway).

A few years later, black leader **Dr. John Dupuis** would start the White Belt Dairy at 61st Street in Lemon City, which, at the time had a greater population than the fledgling city of Miami.

Wilson A. "Sam" Larkins

Hurricane Donna destroyed Lemon City in 1960.

West of Hialeah, Miami Lakes was all dairy land owned by the Graham family. Mining engineer and former Florida State Senator, **Ernest "Cap" Graham** started dairy farming on 3,000 acres after the 1926 Hurricane completely flooded his sugarcane fields.

While oldest son, **Philip Graham**, became publisher of the *Washington Post* and *Newsweek*, and youngest son, **Robert S. "Bob" Graham**, went onto become a twice-elected Governor of Florida and a U.S. Senator, middle son, **William A. "Bill" Graham** went into the family dairy business in 1949, and played a leadership role in organizing the Independent Dairy Farmers Association, serving as its first president. Under Bill's guidance, the family business expanded into Angus beef cattle, pecan groves, sugarcane, timber and real estate development.

By the 1960s, the Graham brothers formed the Graham Companies and began development of Miami Lakes, following the European concept for self-contained towns. Incorporated in December 2000, Miami Lakes is now home to more than 22,000 residents and 1,700 businesses – with the Graham Companies remaining the town's largest landowner.

Robert S. Graham

William A. Graham

A South Florida staple for more than 70 years, the McArthur Dairy was started by **J. Neville McArthur** on 50 acres of land just west of Hollywood, Florida in 1929, with 20 Jersey cows. By the 1950s, the McArthur Dairy had expanded operations as far north as Palm Beach County and as far south as Perrine. The 1960s saw expansion to the west into Belle Glade and the Lake Okeechobee area, and further south into the Florida Keys.

In 1980, Dean Foods Company purchased the dairy's bottling division, but the farms and real estate remain family-owned. With 16,000 cows, the McArthur Dairy is the largest dairy in the state of Florida and the 5th largest dairy in the United States.

J. Neville McArthur

"The friendly cow all red and white,
I love with all my heart;
She gives me cream with all her might;
To eat with apple tart."
- Robert Louis Stevenson

The Age of Romance

Miami resident **June Cutting** described the '30s as the "Age of Romance." She said, "Young people today just don't know how wonderful it was. You were dressed in a lovely chiffon or organdy gown, had a beautiful life of dancing and dining. Romance was here. All the big bands were here. Business here was great. It was an age of design and romance."

Heywood Broun of *Vanity Fair* described it differently. "Miami is vulgar, noisy, ugly and frantic and you and I can certainly have more fun there than in any spot in all the world."

Heywood Broun

In the years following the Great Depression, Miami and the Beaches fared much better than the rest of the nation, largely due to the growing aviation industry, increased tourism and liberal gambling laws. In fact, in 1933, while much of the country was suffering its worst year, Miami Beach was thriving.

N.B.T. Roney had joined forces with the new management of the Biltmore Hotel in Coral Gables (**George Merrick** having gone bankrupt after the 1929 crash), providing buses between the two hotels so that guests could share the beachfront and the golf course. Then, gambling, a huge national trend that swept the country at the time, got a big boost in Miami when the Florida state legislature legalized pari-mutual betting in 1931, and **Joseph E. Widener**, a "Philadelphia capitalist and sportsman," remodeled the old Jockey Club and turned it into the Hialeah Racetrack.

Joseph E. Widener

The track was so successful that the tourist season became unofficially defined by its racing dates, January 1 through March 15, and two additional tracks, Tropical Park and Gulfstream, were licensed to run at the beginning and end of the Hialeah season in 1935.

By 1936, the area offered more gambling than any other place in the nation and an estimated 600 millionaires spent the winter season in Miami Beach...more than any other resort in the country.

One of the investors in Tropical Park was racketeer **Frank Erickson**, one of Capone's men. At the time, the "Father of the Syndicate," **Jake "Greasy Thumb" Guzik**, New York slot machine czar **Frank Costello**, syndicate boss **Frank "The Enforcer" Nitti**, **Tony "Big Tuna" Accardo**, **"Long" Zuillman** and **Lucky Luciano** were among those who helped Capone run his local operation.

Dutch Shulz and gang members from various other cities also wintered in Miami, along with **Meyer Lansky**, who would eventually become Miami's mob boss and "transform illegal gambling from a neighborhood racket into an interstate enterprise."

Tony Accardo

Dutch Shulz

Lucky Luciano

Frank Costello

Meyer Lansky

Other regulars were **Walter Winchell**, who was a wintertime fixture at the Roney Plaza Gardens from 1930 to the 1960s, **Johnny Weissmuller** of Tarzan fame, who started as a lifeguard at the Biltmore Hotel, and Cuban band leader **Desi Arnaz**, who performed nightly at Miami's Jai Alai.

Desi Arnaz

Walter Winchell

Baseball great **George Herman "Babe" Ruth** began golfing at the Biltmore in 1930, and vacationed regularly in Miami until 1948, when he returned for the last time to recuperate from his third cancer operation.

George Herman "Babe" Ruth

 Walter Winchell *was a real "Stage Door Johnny" and could often be seen in the wee hours of the morning escorting young showgirls from* **Lou Walters'** *famous Latin Quarter nightclub in Miami Beach.*

Some familiar names who became permanent residents in the '30s included washing machine king **Elmer Maytag**, thermostat inventor **Mark Honeywell**, owner of the Yellow Cab Company and Hertz U-Drive founder **John D. Hertz** who lived on Pine Tree Drive, shoe man **Leonard Florsheim**, and dime-store chain mogul **Sebastian Kresge**.

Mark Honeywell

John D. Hertz

Sebastian Kresge
K-Mart Founder

Pals **Gary Oldfield** and **Louis Chevrolet** had been early investors in **Carl Fisher's** Miami Beach and Fisher, who was now employed by the Pancoasts to market the area, invited his other associates in the automotive industry down for a visit. **Harvey Firestone** of Firestone Tires, the four Fisher brothers who built car bodies, Henry Ford's associate, **Charles E. Sorenson**, and General Motor's research head and inventor of the self-starter, **Charles Kettering**, all got sand in their shoes in the 1930s.

Charles Kettering

Harvey Firestone

"Once you get sand in your shoes, you never get it out."
- Damon Runyon

*Today's Fontainebleau Hotel stands on the site of **Harvey Firestone's** magnificent Firestone Estate.*

Murder in Miami

It's February 15, 1933. A guest of **J.C. Penney** (who had a home on Belle Island), President-elect **Franklin Delano Roosevelt** arrives for a rally at Bayfront Park on **Vincent Astor's** yacht and is greeted by 25,000 Miamians. He addresses the cheering crowd from an open convertible, but as he finishes his speech, shots ring out. Roosevelt is unharmed, but five others are wounded, including **Mrs. Joseph H. Gill**, wife of the president of Florida Power & Light Company, **R.G. Gautier**, Mayor of Miami, and visiting Chicago Mayor **Anton Cermak**.

Franklin Delano Roosevelt

 *February 15th marked the anniversary of another assassination attempt; one made in 1877 during the controversial Presidential election between Republican **Rutherford B. Hayes** and Democrat **Samuel J. Tilden**. While the Presidency hung in the balance, dependent upon the electoral votes in Florida, South Carolina and Louisiana, an attempt was made on the life of Republican Louisiana Governor **Stephen Packard**. Fortunately, the governor was able to knock down the gun, aimed at his heart, and the discharged bullet only grazed his knee. The perpetrator was taken into custody and the electoral votes went to Hayes.*

An unemployed bricklayer, **Guiseppe Zangara** is quickly seized, tried, convicted of attempted murder, and sentenced to life in prison. But, when Cermak dies on March 6th, Zangara is tried again and sentenced to death (even though Cermak died from pneumonia and not his gunshot wounds).

Guiseppe Zangara

Anton Cermak

 In **Anton Cermak's** memory, a plaque was placed in Bayfront Park in 1943 which reads, "I'm glad it was me instead of you," supposedly the words spoken by Cermak to Roosevelt immediately after the shooting.

There has been some speculation that Zangara's target may actually have been Cermak, and not Roosevelt. This is largely due to the fact that Cermak, who was "as much a gangster as an elected official," had his police force gun down **Frank "The Enforcer" Nitti** two months earlier in Chicago. Nitti survived the shooting, but when he began recovering from his wounds, Cermak fled to Miami, only to be gunned down by Zangara. Zangara, however, testified that Roosevelt was indeed his target and insisted that he had acted alone. He said he originally planned to go to Washington to assassinate President **Herbert Hoover**, but felt Roosevelt's visit to Miami made him an easier target.

Zangara stuck by that story until he was executed in Florida's electric chair just 33 days after his assassination attempt.

Frank "The Enforcer" Nitti

"You can get more done with a kind word and a gun than with a kind word alone."
- Al Capone

 *FDR's son, **Elliott Roosevelt**, was elected Mayor of Miami Beach in 1965.*

Out With the Old...

...in with the new. New Look. New Blood. New Deal.

Commodore W.J. Matheson

After his inauguration in 1933, **President Roosevelt** launched his controversial New Deal initiatives that created jobs, provided retirement benefits, halted home foreclosures and insured bank deposits throughout the nation, as well as establishing a minimum wage. In Miami, New Deal programs put more than 16,000 Miamians to work building schools, housing, public buildings and parks. Greynolds Park, which has been named a historic site and is now one of three South Florida bird sanctuaries recognized by the National Audubon Society, and the beautiful Matheson Hammocks Park, named for chemical-and-dye manufacturer **Commodore W.J. Matheson**, were both created by the Civilian Conservation Corps during this period. It was Matheson who imported the first coconut palm trees from Trinidad to Miami.

David Fairchild

*Chemist **W. J. Matheson** owned Key Biscayne.*

Both parks were designed by famed landscape architect **William Lyman Phillips,** who also designed the Fairchild Tropical Gardens, named for horticulturist **David Fairchild**, and all of Florida's public parks.

William Lyman Phillips

 Matheson Hammock Park and Fairchild Tropical Gardens are both located on Old Cutler Road in Miami. (Public)

Miami, and particularly Miami Beach, took on a whole new look in the 1930s with a hot new architectural style that was known then as "Moderne" and has come to be known today as Art Deco. Sleek, streamlined hotels with an almost nautical look, painted in soft pastels, many with window "eyebrows" and neon trim, designed to "let in the air and sun," sprang up all over the beach.

While many architects contributed to the hundreds of Art Deco structures that went up in the '30s, three of the most prominent were **Henry Hohauser**, credited with being the originator of "Modernism" in Miami Beach; his arch-rival and biggest competitor **L. Murray Dixon**, who would match Hohauser hotel-for-hotel in a building frenzy; and Chicagoan **Roy F. France**, who was, by far, the most prolific hotel architect of the decade.

Lawrence Murray Dixon

Henry Hohauser

Thanks in large part to the efforts of the Design Preservation League and funding from a handful of visionary local builders, several Art Deco hotels have been renovated and preserved, including Hohauser's Essex House Hotel at 1001 Collins Avenue and his world-famous Clevelander Hotel, 1020 Ocean Drive; **Roy France's** *National Hotel and St. Moritz (now part of the Loews) on Collins Avenue; and* **L. Murray Dixon's** *Tides Hotel on Ocean Drive, Ritz Plaza Hotel, 1701 Collins Avenue, and dual hotels, the McAlpin and the Ocean Plaza, next-door neighbors to the north of* **Henry Hohauser's** *Crescent Hotel, 1420 Ocean Drive.*

Less pretentious and less expensive to build, these new hotels were better suited to the tastes and pocketbooks of the newly arriving middle class, the "working rich," and the new, predominantly Jewish blood that began visiting and settling in the area.

Al Jolson

Eddie Cantor, George Jessel and **Al Jolson,** who had a home on the Venetian Islands, provided local entertainment, as did comedian **Joe Lewis** and American icon **Tom Mix.**

Eddie Cantor

Tom Mix &
Tony, the Wonder Horse

The larger, more elegant Mediterranean-style hotels like the Nautilus, the Flamingo and the Roney Plaza, continued to attract the rich and famous, and Chalk's Ocean Airways regularly catered to such notables as **Judy Garland**, **Errol Flynn**, **Ernest Hemingway** and **Howard Hughes**, who had a home on Sunset Island.

Howard Hughes

Judy Garland

Ernest Hemingway

Errol Flynn

Amelia Earhart

By 1935, Eastern was making daily flights between Miami, New York, Chicago and intermediate cities, and Pan American Airlines was making regular flights to 32 South American countries, bringing an influx of Latin Americans to the city. **Charles Lindbergh**, himself, came down to Miami in the '30s to inspect the Pan Am operation and would retire here. And it was from Miami or, more specifically, Hialeah, that famed aviator **Amelia Earhart** and navigator **Fred Noonan**, a former Pan Am pilot, left on their ill-fated trip around the world on June 1, 1937, disappearing over the Pacific Ocean one month later.

Charles Lindbergh

*Beautiful **Amelia Earhart** Park, located on 450 acres at Palm Avenue and 62nd St. in Hialeah, offers a multitude of family fun, including the Graham Dairy's Petting Zoo, a roller-skating park, rock garden, pony rides and more.*

In 1936, **Irving Berlin's** *Moon Over Miami* was #1 on the Hit Parade and, in 1941, a movie of the same name was made starring **Betty Grable** and **Don Ameche**. It succeeded in painting an exotic picture of a tropical paradise abounding with beautiful people living the good life in "America's Playground," even though the entire picture was made on a Hollywood back lot.

Irving Berlin

On July 15, 1939, the heavily drinking **Carl Fisher** died of a gastric hemorrhage, complicated by cirrhosis of the liver. His epitaph in the *Miami Daily News* read, "Carl G. Fisher, who looked at a piece of swampland and visualized the nation's greatest winter playground, died...in the city of his fulfilled dreams." He was 65.

"Adventure is worthwhile in itself."
- Amelia Earhart

Marching Through Time

Troops marching down Collins Avenue, 1942

Camp Miami Beach

On December 7, 1941, the Sunday *Miami Herald* predicted that Miami would have the best tourist season in history. At 2:30 p.m. that same day, the Japanese bombed Pearl Harbor.

Florida's strategic location made it vital for national defense and, in February 1942, 4,000 officers-in-training were sent to Miami Beach by the Army Air Corps under the command of **Lt. Col. James S. Stowell.**

More than 40 ships were torpedoed off of Florida's Atlantic coast early that year and, on May 14, German submarines torpedoed a neutral Mexican tanker eight miles off of Virginia Key, just south of Miami Beach. Burning out of control, the doomed vessel drifted northward for several hours in full view of the beach's horrified residents.

Tourism was immediately restricted, blackouts were enforced, and Miami's abundant hotels and restaurants became ready-made barracks and mess halls for our military troops. The Biltmore and Nautilus Hotels were used as hospitals, the DuPont Building (dubbed the U.S.S. Neversink) became the Navy's Gulf Sea Frontier headquarters, and the Bay Shore Golf Course became "Camp Miami Beach."

More than 1/4 of all the officers and 1/5 of all the enlisted men in the entire Army Air Forces of WWII trained in Miami Beach; more than 500,000 troops and 50,000 officers.

Recruits at Bay Shore Golf Club

South Floridians did their part in the war effort, raising more than $145,000,000 in war bonds, largely through the efforts of people like long-time Miami Beach resident and community activist **Rose Weiss**. Rose, who was affectionately known as the "Mother of Miami Beach," personally sold more than $5 million in war bonds.

Rose Weiss

Arthur B. "Pappy" Chalk
Founder
Chalk's Ocean Airways

Arthur B. Chalk donated his planes and service to the Civil Air Patrol, assisted in training Navy seaplane pilots, and personally flew hundreds of anti-submarine missions off the coast.

Mitchell Wolfson, co-founder of the Wometco Theater chain as well as Miami's first television station, WTVJ Channel 4, became Miami Beach's first Jewish mayor in June 1943, but resigned a few months later to accept a commission as a major in the Army Specialist Reserve.

Mitchell Wolfson, Sr.

 Mitchell Wolfson was originally from Key West.

Bob Hope

Kay Pancoast (who was married to **John Collins'** grandson, architect **Russell Pancoast**) and **Zoe P. Renshaw**, wife of Miami Beach's city manager, organized the Miami Beach Pier Association; a recreation facility for the servicemen that enlisted more than 18,000 volunteers.

Danny Kaye

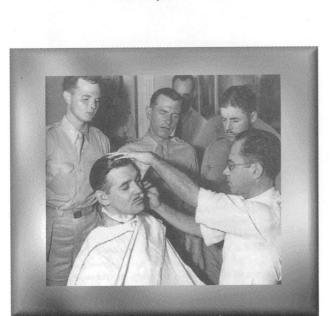

Clark Gable

Clark Gable was an officer-in-training and regular "G.I. Joe" living in the barracks in Miami Beach, and **Bob Hope, Danny Kaye, Rita Hayworth** and **Orson Welles** entertained the troops.

With sand firmly lodged in their shoes, Gable and Hope both continued to spend their winters in Miami Beach after the war.

Even Miami mob boss, **Meyer Lansky**, did his patriotic duty. It is said he acted as liaison between **Lucky Luciano** and the U.S. military in enlisting the Italian Mafia's help in the American invasion of Sicily.

Meyer Lansky

More than 4,600 Floridians serving in the armed forces died during the war; 515 were from Miami. The war's first Medal of Honor was awarded to **Lieutenant Alexander Ninninger** of Ft. Lauderdale for leading a counterattack against the Japanese on Bataan. (He didn't survive the conflict.) And it was Miamian **Paul W. Tibbits, Jr.** who commanded the B-29 bomber, the **Enola Gay** (named for his mother who was, herself, a Miami resident), who dropped the first atomic bomb over Hiroshima in August 1945.

One week later, the Japanese surrendered.

Paul W. Tibbets, Jr.

"Grimly, earnestly and willingly, Miami assumed the mantle of a community at war."
                                                                    - John Pennekamp

 *Before the war, **Paul Tibbets, Jr.** had a job which required him to fly over the Hialeah Racetrack and drop advertising flyers.*

A Piece of the Action

Although the tourist industry collapsed during the war, the government compensated for much of these losses and Miami continued to prosper. Gambling at local racetracks reached an all-time high, and everybody wanted "a piece of the action."

Frank Erickson, with his ties to **Frank Costello** and **Al Capone**, ran Miami's largest bookmaking operation, and brothers **Meyer** and **Jake Lansky** were operating big casinos in both Dade and Broward Counties.

Frank Costello

"Trigger Mike" Coppola

Out-of-town talent included some of the underworld's most notorious gamblers and racketeers; **Joe Adonis**, **Alfred "Big Al" Polizzi**, **"Trigger Mike" Coppola** (who owned a home on Alton Road) and **Vincent Alo** (also known as Jimmie Blue Eyes). Infamous mobsters **Anthony Carfano** and **James Plumieri** from New York, and Gambino family associate **Joseph "Chicky" Chierico** from Ohio also got in on the action.

Vincent "Jimmy Blue Eyes" Alo

Joe Adonis

Jimmy Plumieri had a home in Surfside.

Meyer Lansky lived in the Imperial House Condominiums on Collins Avenue until his death on May 15, 1983. Acquitted of income tax evasion in 1973, his net worth at the time of his death was estimated at more than $400 million.

In 1944, tired of fighting the competition, Miami Beach bookmakers **Sam Cohen, Jules Levitt, Harold Salvey** (who owned several hotels in Sunny Isles), **Charlie Friedman** and **Eddie Rosenbaum** banded together and formed their own cartel, the S&G Syndicate, and went into the business of financing other bookmakers.

Going into partnership with the hotel builders, actually holding a piece of the mortgage, the S&G was able to place bookmaking concessions in every one of their hotels. By 1948, they controlled more than 200 bookmaking operations in 65 Miami Beach properties, becoming the biggest criminal organization in the South.

A war between Capone's mob and the S&G ensued. There was no shooting in the streets, but raids were launched, communications thwarted, politicians were bought and sold, and local law enforcement looked the other way, or were "in the pockets" of one syndicate or the other.

S&G Syndicate
(Left to Right) Jules Levitt, lawyer Ben Cohen, Edward Rosenbaum,
Harold Salvey and Leo Levitt

In 1947, when **Frank Erickson's** men paid off hotel owner **Meyer Schine** and took over control of the Roney Plaza, Chief of Police **Phil Short** personally conducted the raid against Erickson on instructions from the S&G.

The next year, financial contributions from Jacksonville dog track owner **Bill Johnston**, one of Capone's men, put **Fuller Warren** in the governor's seat. Warren then appointed shady P.I. **W.O. Crosby** to investigate Miami's gambling syndicates, and Crosby, along with Dade County Sheriff **"Smiling Jimmy" Sullivan**, conducted raids against the S&G.

Jimmy Sullivan

When Miami Beach city councilman and municipal judge **Melvin J. Richard** returned at war's end, he was shocked to find the entire city under the influence of the gambling syndicate. He enlisted the aid of former FBI agent **Daniel Sullivan**, operating director of the Crime Commission of Greater Miami and, together, they relentlessly pursued the S&G, despite an array of bribes and threats.

Even when **Harry "The Muscle" Russell**, a front man for Capone, became a 1/6 partner in the S&G in 1950, thereby "upping the stakes," **Mel Richard** was not deterred.

Melvin J. Richard

Daniel Sullivan

 *Mel Richard's son was the attorney who represented **George W. Bush** in the 2000 Presidential election when "hanging chads" hung up the Presidency of the United States.*

Then, one of the letters Richard had written to his senator was passed onto Tennessee Senator **Estes Kefauver**, who chaired the U.S. Senate's Special Committee to Investigate Crime in Interstate Commerce. In July, Miami had the dubious honor of becoming the first of 14 American cities to be investigated by the Committee.

Senator Estes Kefauver

It put the S&G out of business and ended the political careers of Governor **Fuller Warren**, Dade County Sheriff **Jimmy Sullivan**, and Broward County Sheriff **Walter Clark**.

Local operations moved to Las Vegas and Havana. Open gambling in Miami was over.

"Gambling. The sure way of getting nothing for something."
- Wilson Mizner

Middle-Class Miami

Many of the men and women who had trained in Miami Beach got "sand in their shoes" and returned to settle permanently after the war. Having lost the aura of exclusivity partially attained in the '30s, by 1950, Miami's population had more than doubled and was now solidly middle-class. Automobiles, airplanes and, "necessity being the mother of invention," the advent of air-conditioning, contributed significantly to this growth.

The ban on construction that had been in effect during the war was lifted and more new hotels were built in Greater Miami between 1945 and 1954 than in all the other states combined.

The most spectacular of these new hotels were the magnificent 565-room Fontainebleau Hotel with its "stairway to nowhere" and its next-door neighbor, the equally opulent Eden Roc. Both, often criticized, hotels were designed by Russian-born architect **Morris Lapidus**, who felt that tourists came to Miami Beach to be entertained and wanted his hotels, themselves, to be part of the entertainment.

Morris Lapidus

 Born in 1902, Morris Lapidus lived in the same condominium in Miami's Belle Meade area near the Venetian Causeway for more than 40 years. He died on January 18, 2001, at the age of 98.

Lapidus' "...too much is never enough" attitude earned him a reputation for "superschlock," but the tourists loved it, and celebrities like **Frank Sinatra, Dean Martin, Jerry Lewis** and **Liberace** performed at both hotels. **Steve Allen** even broadcast his "Tonight Show" from the Fontainebleau's "La Ronde Room" in 1957.

Frank Sinatra

Dean Martin & Jerry Lewis

 Jerry Lewis' movie, "The Bellboy" was filmed at the Fontainebleau Hotel in 1960.

Meanwhile, further north, **Shepard Broad** created a new community by connecting two islands with a causeway, Bay Harbor Islands. This opened the way for development in Bal Harbour, Surfside, Sunny Isles and Golden Beach.

Later, other prominent builders came to Bal Harbour, including Chicagoan **Sol Taplin**, who built the Harbour House, Bal Harbour's first luxury high-rise.

Sol was also one of the Founders of the Shul of Bal Harbour...in a town that had previously been restricted to Jews.

Shepard Broad

Sol M. Taplin

 *In the early '50s, legendary deli man **Wolfie Cohen** moved his restaurant to Sunny Isles. Still a Miami Beach landmark, **Wolfie Cohen's** Rascal House is now owned by California-based Jerry's Famous Deli.*

In 1955, **Arthur Godfrey**, aka "The Old Redhead," began broadcasting his radio and television shows from the Kenilworth Hotel in Bal Harbour. These weekly broadcasts brought middle-class Miami into the homes of middle-class America.

Arthur Godfrey

 During WWII, Bal Harbour was the site of an Army Air Corps rifle range as well as a German P.O.W. camp.

 Godfrey generated so much publicity for Miami that 41st Street was named in his honor, Arthur Godfrey Road.

Picking up the baton, television and talk-show host **Larry King** began his career in Miami as a disc jockey and sports commentator for WAHR in 1957 and WKAT in 1958.

Miami's *Pumpernik Restaurant* became Larry's next venue, where he interviewed "whoever happened to be there at the time" for a rag sheet called *The Miami Beach Sun*. This led to a WIOD contract and King's career skyrocketed until his ostentatious lifestyle and big spending left him seriously in debt and he was charged with grand larceny, accused of stealing $5,000 from a business partner.

Although King was found not-guilty of all charges in 1972, the scandal nearly cost him his career. He moved to Shreveport, Louisiana to be the color commentator for the short-lived Shreveport Steamers of the World Football League.

In 1975, WIOD rehired King for an evening interview show and he gradually recovered his career, although he continued his free-spending lifestyle.

On January 30, 1978, the *Larry King Show* debuted in 28 cities and remains one of the highest rated talk shows on the air today.

Larry King

"Upper classes are a nation's past; the middle class is its future."
- **Ayn Rand**

Big Business

War is good for business. **Henry Flagler** knew that back in 1898.

When the *U.S.S. Maine* was sunk in Havana Harbor during the Spanish-American War, it was Flagler who convinced the government to send 7,500 troops to "Camp Miami," and transported them down on his railroad.

The troops needed to be clothed and **William Burdine,** who had a dry goods store in Polk County, and his son, **Roddey,** supplied this service. The newly formed Wm. Burdine and Son Department Store and other local businesses thrived as Flagler had anticipated, but the 1,200 outnumbered Miami residents were terrorized by the bored soldiers, miserable from the heat and lack of facilities to accommodate them. The situation became so explosive that it came to be known as the "Battle of Miami." Fortunately, to the relief of the soldiers and residents alike, the war ended quickly and the troops were only too happy to leave; one soldier writing, "If I owned both Miami and Hell, I'd rent out Miami and live in Hell."

William Burdine

Roddey Burdine

 *The Orange Bowl Stadium, which was completed in 1937, was originally named the **Roddey Burdine** Stadium. It became the Orange Bowl in 1959.*

 "Camp Miami" was located rooughly on the site of today's Bayside Marketplace.

During World War II, many local businesses became huge conglomerates as well, among them Ryder (Truck Company).

Founded by **James A. Ryder** in 1933, with only one $35 *Model A* Ford truck, by 1949, Ryder expanded operations to five branches and 450 trucks, and revenues topped $1 million.

With sand in his shoes and sand in his tires, Ryder is still based in Miami and today, boasts sales of more than $5 billion annually with operations throughout the world.

James A. Ryder

Two of South Florida's largest food chains also experienced huge expansions during the war years. The **Davis** brothers, **Artemus Darius, James Elsworth, Milton Austin** and **Tine Wayne**, turned a single grocery store in Miami into one of the nation's largest supermarket chains with the purchase of the 73-store Winn & Lovett Grocery Co. It became Winn-Dixie and has expanded to more than 1,000 stores in 14 states and the Bahamas, ranking as the ninth largest supermarket chain in the nation.

The Davis Brothers
Austin, A.D., Tine and J.E.
Founders
Winn-Dixie

So, too, the first Publix Food Store was opened by **George W. Jenkins** in 1930. By war's end, Jenkins had purchased a chain of 19 small grocery stores and, in 1948, he started to replace these stores with "supermarkets." Today, Publix has more than 700 stores in Florida, Georgia, South Carolina, Alabama and Tennessee. With 120,000 associates, it is one of the fastest growing employee-owned companies in the United States.

George W. Jenkins
Founder
Publix Food Stores

 One of the Jenkins family members still lives in Bay Harbor Islands.

"Fast food" became a big business in South Florida, as well, when Miami residents **James W. McLamore** and **David Edgerton** founded *Burger King of Miami, Inc.* (originally *Insta Burger King*) in 1954, and made Miami the "Home of the Whopper" in 1957. By 1961, *Burger King* had 45 outlets located throughout Florida and the southeast and acquired national franchise rights.

Sold to *Pillsbury* in 1967, in 1972 the name was changed to the *Burger King Corporation* which today operates more than 11,350 restaurants in 58 countries and territories worldwide; 91% of which are owned and operated by independent franchisees.

On December 11, 2002, the *Burger King Corporation* opened its new world headquarters located at the Waterford Office complex at 5505 Blue Lagoon Drive, near Miami International Airport.

Two days later, on "Friday the 13th", with annual sales topping $11.3 billion, *Burger King* was sold to a group of investors led by the *Texas Pacific Group* for $1.5 billion.

James W. McLamore

 James McLamore of Burger King led a capital campaign that raised $519 million for the University of Miami.

Another "fast food" giant, long-time South Florida resident, **Dave Thomas,** founder of the *Wendy's Old Fashioned Hamburger* chain, started his first restaurant in 1969, in Columbus, Ohio, and personally promoted his "hot and juicy" burgers by appearing in over 500 television commercials; more than any other celebrity.

Today, there are more than 6,000 *Wendy's* restaurants in the United States and 34 countries, with $7 billion in annual sales.

Thomas's true passion, however, was in helping adopted children find loving homes. Adopted himself, he founded the Dave Thomas Foundation for Adoption in 1992, and contributed much of his time and fortune to this cause.

Dave Thomas died in his Fort Lauderdale home on January 8, 2002. He was 69.

Dave Thomas

Tony Roma

Lum's, the "fast food" chain famous for its hot dogs cooked in beer, also got its start in Miami in 1956, by **Clifford** and **Stuart Perlman.** Their first restaurant was little more than a bar located on 41st Street (Arthur Godfrey Road).

With the monies earned from the famous franchise, the Perlman's would later buy Caesar's Palace in Las Vegas in 1969 for $60 million, and over the following ten years would expand Caesar's World, Inc. into a half-billion dollar gaming empire.

Another restaurant mogul who found fame and fortune in South Florida was **Tony Roma**. Roma built his first "Famous for Ribs" restaurant in North Miami Beach in 1972 – and ribs weren't even on the original menu! What began as a weekend special eventually became Roma's signature fare.

When *Cowboy's* owner **Clint Murchison, Jr.,** in Miami for the 1976 Super Bowl, dined at the restaurant, he was so enamored of the cuisine that he purchased the franchise rights for the restaurant from Roma. He retained the name – and Roma's secret recipe.

Today, there are more than 260 *Tony Roma's* in 27 countries, including Europe, Japan, Australia, the Caribbean and Central and South America, as well as throughout the United States.

"Where's the Beef?" During the Civil War, South Florida was the largest beef provider for the Confederate Army.

Milton Berle was the national spokesman for Lum's.

Milton Berle once joked, "If opportunity doesn't knock, build a door," and many of Miami's most successful businessmen did just that; they built doors – and walls – and roofs – and roads – and schools – and hospitals – and hotels.

Building has always been, and continues to be, very big business in Miami.

Some of the most notable builders in recent years include: **Stephen Muss,** a well-known Miamian and real estate mogul who bought the Fontainebleau Hotel in 1978 for $28 million after it had been forced into bankruptcy, and restored it to its former glory at a cost of another $30 million;

Stephen Muss

Arthur Vining Davis, an aluminum magnate (ALCOA) who came to Florida in 1948, and proceeded to buy up huge portions of land in South Dade and along North Kendall Drive. The resultant Arvida Corporation was responsible for the development of most of today's Kendall area as well as Baptist Hospital and the Palmetto Expressway; and

Arthur Vining Davis

*Stephen Muss's wife, **Sandra**, was once married to disgraced financier **David Paul**, CEO of the now-defunct Centrust Savings and Loan.*

Leonard Miller, founder of the Lennar Corporation, who settled in Miami in 1956 with his wife **Susan.** Starting with capital of only $10,000, Miller began building homes, eventually expanding his holdings from Florida to California, Texas, Arizona, New Jersey, Maryland, Virginia, Minnesota, Colorado, North Carolina, Michigan and Ohio.

While Davis passed away in 1962, and Miller died in 2002, Muss is still building. Along with his daughter, **Melanie Muss,** and Turnberry Associates Principal **Jeffrey Soffer** (Turnberry Associates Managing Partner **Don Soffer's** son), he's building an ultra-exclusive $200 million 36-story luxury condominium hotel at the south end of the Fontainebleau property.

Leonard Miller

Robert M. Swedroe

Jeffrey Soffer

Turnberry's architect, **Robert M. Swedroe,** came to the area in 1960, and served as senior designer for Miami icon **Morris Lapidus** for more than a decade before starting his own architectural firm in 1974. With his innovative space planning designs and use of direct access elevators, Swedroe took vertical living in Miami to a whole new level.

Another long-time Miami builder, **Martin Z. Margulies,** who built the *Grand Bay Towers* on Key Biscayne, *Grove Isle* in Coconut Grove and *The Kenilworth* in Bal Harbour, continues to build, recently completing another luxury high-rise condominium in Bal Harbour, the magnificant *Bellini on the Ocean.*

Also an avid art collector, **Marty Margulies** was recently rated by *Art in America Magazine* as one of the top 200 art collectors in the world.

Martin Z. Margulies and Martin W. Taplin

Combining the building business with the art business, Miami developer and financier **Martin W. Taplin** and his wife, **Christine "Cricket" Taplin** display their personal rotating collection of contemporary art in Taplin's trendy new *Sagamore Hotel* located in the heart of Miami's South Beach. Cricket curates the collection.

Next door to **Ian Schrager's** world-famous *Delano, The Sagamore,* which frequent guest rapper **Sean "P Diddy" Combs** described as being "in a zone by its own," is setting a new trend in boutique hotels. Diddy even filmed his "Down For Me" music video at *The Sagamore.*

Ian Schrager

Following ex-gal pal **Jennifer Lopez's** lead, Diddy also got sand in his shoes. He recently purchased record mogul **Tommy Mottola's** estate on Star Island.

Ian Schrager also has family living in Miami.

 Ian Schrager was the former co-owner of New York City's infamous Studio 54 nightclub at the height of its popularity in the 1970s.

Cricket and Marty Taplin
in the Lobby of the
Sagamore Hotel

Another one of the world's top 200 art collectors, **Norman Braman**, who owns several large auto dealerships in Florida and was also the former owner of the Philadelphia Eagles football team, joined forces with several other major Miami art collectors in an effort to bring the world's most acclaimed art fair from Basel, Switzerland to Miami Beach.

Delayed by the September 11th attacks, *Art Basel Miami Beach* made its debut in December 2002, bringing with it the global arts media, art collectors from all over the world, and international recognition and acclaim.

Norman Braman

Not limited to North American businesses, four of the 100 largest Hispanic-owned companies in the world are located in Miami; hospital supplier Pharmed Corp. (founded by **Carlos** and **Jorge de Cespedes**), cell phone distributor Brightstar Corp. (CEO **R. Marcelo Claure**), telecom builder MasTec Inc. (founded by **Jorge Mas Canosa** who died in 1997), and real estate developer The Related Group of Florida (chairman **Jorge M. Perez**). In addition, Miami-based UNIVISION is the nation's largest Hispanic television network and the *El Nuevo Herald,* the Spanish language version of the *Miami Herald,* has the largest circulation of any daily Spanish newspaper in the United States.

Carlos & Jorge de Cespedes
Pharmed Corp.

Jorge M. Perez
The Related Group of Florida

Jorge Mas Canosa
MasTec, Inc.

There's big business...and then there's really big business.

Several of the nation's top 500 *billionaires* live in South Florida, including **Micky Arison,** chairman of Miami-based Carnival Corp., Miami-native **Jeff Bezos,** founder of Amazon.com, and entrepreneur **H. Wayne Huizenga, Jr.**, owner of Ft. Lauderdale-based AutoNation and Waste Management Company, to name but a few, proving the old adage that, *"the chief business of the American people is business."*

Micky Arison
Carnival Corp.

H. Wayne Huizenga, Jr.
AutoNation
Waste Management Company

Jeff Bezos
Amazon.com

"Money never starts an idea; it is the idea that starts the money."
- W.J. Cameron

Waterlogged

South of the city, another community to thrive throughout the 1940s and '50s was the unique community of shacks built on piles driven into the shallow Biscayne Bay bottom, known today as Stiltsville.

Begun in the 1930s, and some say as early as 1922, Stiltsville's first permanent resident was a fisherman and former lighthouse keeper named **"Crawfish Eddie" (or "Crawfish Charlie") Walker,** so nicknamed for the crawfish chowder he made and sold from his shack on the water. He was soon joined by pals **Thomas Grady**, who was the city's rate and traffic consultant, **L.L. Lee**, the city manager, and **Leo Edwards**, an automobile dealer – and Stiltsville was born.

Accessible only by boat, some early structures being nothing more than sunken barges, generators supplied the electricity, water was brought in jugs, and human waste had to be returned to shore in barrels.

In 1940, Stiltsville's first private club opened, **Ed Turner's** *Quarterdeck Club*, followed soon after by *The Swan*, later renamed the *Probus*. Alcohol, gambling and prostitution abounded and the country club atmosphere made Stiltsville the place to be for Miami's social elite and those hoping to join their ranks.

Commodore Edward Turner

During the war, one of the shacks, owned by Miami attorney **Joseph Weintraub**, was used as a Coast Guard Auxiliary headquarters. After the war, Stiltsville flourished, even electing its own unofficial mayor, realtor **Jimmy Ellenburg**.

By 1960, there were 27 structures in Stiltsville owned by Miami businessmen, bankers, airplane pilots, developers and hoteliers.

Surviving Hurricane Betsy in 1965 and Hurricane Andrew in 1992, today only seven shacks remain.

Now a part of Biscayne National Park, privately owned leases on the properties have expired leaving their future undetermined. Too new to be considered historic by the National Register of Historic Places since the remaining structures were built after 1960's Hurricane Donna, advocates like Miami Rep. **Ileana Ros-Lehtinen** (R-Fla) are fighting to keep this historic community afloat as "a salty reminder of Miami's seafaring past" and a "time-worn testament to a slower, simpler time."

Ileana Ros-Lehtinen

 *Governor **Thomas LeRoy Collins** was a frequent guest aboard **Jimmy Ellenburg's** yacht in the 1950s.*

Further south across the water trouble was brewing in Havana. In 1959, Cuban dictator **Fulgencio Batista** was driven out of power by the newly formed Marxist government led by a man named **Fidel Castro**. In the years ahead, the resultant exodus of more than a half-million Cubans fleeing Castro's tyranny would transform Miami from a resort town into an international city.

Fidel Castro

"Water, water, everywhere,
And all the boards did shrink;
Water, water, everywhere,
Nor any drop to drink."
- Samuel Taylor Coleridge, *"The Rime of the Ancient Mariner"*

Former Dictator Batista had real estate in Miami Beach.

*After he lost a fortune in the communist takeover of Cuba where he had substantial holdings, **Meyer Lansky** offered a $1 million reward for the capture or death of Cuban Dictator **Fidel Castro**; there were no takers.*

The Good, The Bad,
The Ugly
and
The Bizarre

Louis F. Snedigear
Miami Beach Mayor
with sand in his shoes
(and sand in his shorts)

The Winds of Change

The '60s folk group *Peter, Paul and Mary* captured the essence of the times with their poignant tune, "Blowin' in the Wind."

Miamians took their words literally when two major hurricanes ripped through the city changing the face of Miami forever. Hurricane Donna barreled through in 1960, followed by the even-more devastating Hurricane Betsy in 1965. However, their turbulent winds were nothing in comparison to the winds of change that swept through Florida and the rest of the nation during the '50s and '60s.

Again, Miami's location put it in the eye of the storm.

These were serious times with serious issues and serious players.

John F. Kennedy

The influx of Cuban immigrants, the failed Bay of Pigs invasion, the Cuban Missile Crisis which brought our country to the brink of war, and Miami's first race riots – serious times.

Santo Trafficante, Jr.

Seen in Miami: President **John F. Kennedy** and his brother, Attorney General **Robert Kennedy**, Teamsters boss **Jimmy Hoffa**, mobster **Santo Trafficante, Jr.**, Richard M. Nixon and **Fidel Castro** – serious players.

Miami was no stranger to the Kennedy brothers. Their parents, **Joe** and **Rose Kennedy**, lived in Miami Beach's *Altos del Mar* while their home in Palm Beach was being built and, before Jack became President, the brothers and their friends would often cruise Biscayne Bay off Miami Beach, away from the prying eyes and ears of the press.

Jimmy Hoffa

Jimmy Hoffa lived in Bay Harbor Islands in a luxury apartment building that is said to have been financed by the Teamsters.

In Florida, one of the men who dealt with these serious issues and helped transform *Old Florida* into the *New South* was **Thomas LeRoy Collins**.

A state legislator by the age of 25, Collins was elected Governor in 1954 to serve out the term of his predecessor **Dan McCarty**, who had died in office of a heart attack. Re-elected in 1956, he became the first Florida governor in modern times to win two consecutive terms.

Thomas LeRoy Collins

Under the 1964 Civil Rights Act, Collins became director of the Community Relations Service and in 1965, negotiated a peaceful resolution to a national civil rights march led by **Dr. Martin Luther King, Jr.** Because of Collins' unwavering belief that "segregation is morally wrong," Florida experienced only minimal disorder during the desegregation process, unlike many other southern states.

In 1965, he was branded a race-mixer, agitator and liberal when he was photographed in Selma walking with **Dr. Martin Luther King, Jr., Andrew Young** and **Ralph Abernathy**. It cost him the 1968 Senate election, but Collins went on to spend the next 23 years practicing law and passionately speaking out against "racial injustice everywhere in the United States" and the death penalty, firmly standing by his belief that, "Murder by the state is still murder."

*A proponent for education, **Thomas LeRoy Collins** created Florida's first community colleges. Miami-Dade Community College (known then as Dade Junior College) opened in 1960.*

The assassination of **John F. Kennedy** in 1963 and the assassinations of **Dr. Martin Luther King, Jr.** and **Robert Kennedy** in 1968, split the nation in two. Disillusioned, many young people turned to illegal, mind-altering drugs and, as it had been during Prohibition for the bootleggers, South Florida's extensive coastline became safe haven for drug traffickers. Incredible amounts of money poured into Miami and hordes of long-haired "flower children" descended on Coconut Grove's Peacock Park, making it resemble San Francisco's Haight-Ashbury, the hippie capital of the world.

Race riots raged throughout the country and **President Lyndon B. Johnson's** urban renewal programs further incensed Miami's Blacks when construction of I-95 cut through the center of Overtown, once a model community. Forced to relocate to overcrowded ghettos mostly in Liberty City, unbearable overcrowding and substandard housing and facilities, coupled with Miami's oppressive heat, exploded in Miami's first race riot which erupted during **Richard Nixon's** Republican National Convention in August 1968, and lasted for three days.

Sadly, it would not be its last.

Dr. Martin Luther King, Jr.

Lyndon B. Johnson

"Change your thoughts and you change your world."
- Norman Vincent Peale

Bad Boys

Being a major metropolitan city with a diverse population, Miami is often in the news when the news is bad – and sometimes the bad news is simply the result of men behaving badly.

In the mid-1960s, middle-weight boxing champion **Jake LaMotta** was jailed in Miami for trafficking in teenage sex; introducing 14-year-old minor girls to his friends in social clubs.

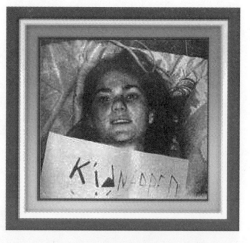

A few years later, in 1968, Miami land developer **Robert Mackle's** daughter **Barbara** was kidnapped at gunpoint and buried underground in a wooden box for 3-1/2 days, sparking one of the largest manhunts in FBI history. Fortunately, the kidnappers, University of Miami researcher **Gary Steven Krist** and his accomplice **Ruth Eiseman-Schier,** gave Mackle his daughter's location after Mackle paid a $500,000 ransom.

Barbara was found, dehydrated but alive.

Barbara Mackle

Krist and Schier were later arrested; Shier serving three years in prison before being deported to her native Honduras, and Krist only serving 10 years of his life sentence.

Ruth Eiseman-Schier

Gary Steven Krist

Incredibly, after being released from prison, Krist earned himself a medical degree and in December of 2001, was actually granted a probationary medical license by the state of Indiana – pending regular psychiatric reviews.

*The blockbuster movie, "Raging Bull," was modeled after **Jake LaMotta's** life in New York and Miami. He lived in Altos del Mar at 77th & Collins.*

The Mackle brothers developed Key Biscayne.

Another bad girl, **Joyce Cohen** was convicted of murdering her husband, Miami builder **Stanley Cohen**, in 1986. She was sentenced to life in prison without the possibility of parole.

One year later, in another high-profile assassination, Cigarette boat designer **Donald Aronow** was killed gangland style as he sat parked in his car. Said to have had close ties with **Meyer Lansky**, the "untouchable" Mafia chief who roamed Miami Beach at will for over 50 years, Aronow's murder has never been solved.

If "power corrupts and absolute power corrupts absolutely" and "the love of money is the root of all evil," then surely "the line separating power and greed is very fine."

Power and greed were significant motivators for two of our city's highest profile white collar bad boys, **David Paul**, disgraced former Chairman and CEO of the now defunct Centrust Savings and Loan, and **Victor Posner**, millionaire corporate raider.

While Paul was sentenced to 11 years in prison (he was just recently released) and ordered to pay a whopping $65 million in fines and restitution on fraud and racketeering charges, including pilfering millions of dollars from the bank to decorate his $10 million waterfront estate on LaGorce Island, Posner only had to pay $3 million in restitution for tax evasion and serve 5,000 hours of community service.

Victor Posner

Master of the hostile takeover, Posner, the former owner of *Arby's*, *Royal Crown Cola* and *Sharon Steel*, among others, drove many of his companies into bankruptcy while simultaneously drawing millions of dollars in annual salaries from these same corporations.

In 1988, Victor and his son were accused of conspiring with junk bond kings **Ivan Boesky** and **Michael Milken**, in an attempt to conceal a plan to seize control of the Fischbach Corporation electrical company. While Boesky and Milken both pled guilty to the charges and were sent to prison, the Posners got off with a "slap on the wrist," ordered only to pay an additional $4 million in restitution to Fischbach and both being banned by the SEC from any further involvement with any public company – ever.

Donald Aronow lived on North Bay Road.

David Paul was a former director of Calvin Klein.

Victor Posner was a self-made millionaire by the age of 25. When he died in February 2002, his fortune was estimated at somewhere between $200 and $500 million. Had had homes on Sunset Island and Golden Beach.

In 1972, five men were arrested in an apparent espionage raid on the Democratic National Committee Headquarters at the Watergate Hotel in Washington, D.C. All five had past CIA connections and had been involved in anti-Castro activities in Florida. Four of the five men were from Miami.

The leader of the group, **Bernard L. Barker**, was a Miami realtor. A former CIA operative, Barker had also served in General Batista's secret police before the Cuban revolution and, as a member of Brigade 2506, survived the ill-fated Bay of Pigs invasion in 1961. Aside from coordinating the break-in, Barker was also the money man in the operation.

Virgilio R. Gonzalez was a Miami locksmith who also served in Brigade 2506, surviving the Bay of Pigs invasion, as was **Eugenio R. Martinez**, a licensed real estate agent and notary public who worked for **Bernard Barker's** real estate firm.

James W. McCord, Jr., aka **Edward Martin**, was a CIA operative at the time of the Bay of Pigs invasion. As security coordinator for the Republican National Committee and the Committee for the Re-election of the President, McCord was responsible for "fingering" the President, stating in a letter to Judge **John Sirica,** who presided over the investigation, that "higher-ups" had approved the break-in.

Bernard L. Barker

Frank Sturgis

James W. McCord, Jr.

Virgilio Gonzalez

Eugenio R. Martinez

E. Howard Hunt, Jr.

Frank Sturgis was among those questioned by the FBI after the death of John Kennedy because of his ties to Permindex, David Ferrie and the entire Miami-Houston-Havana group named in the investigation.

The fifth man, **Frank A. Sturgis**, aka **Frank Fiorini**, had served in Cuban Military Army Intelligence and headed an international anti-Communist brigade after the Bay of Pigs invasion that trained Cuban exiles in guerrilla operations. He also had CIA ties.

Both Barker and Martinez were carrying the phone number of CIA agent **Howard Hunt** at the time of their arrest.

So, too, **E. Howard Hunt**, a long-time CIA operative, sometime White House consultant and mystery novelist, was indicted in the Watergate scandal along with a defiant **G. Gordon Liddy**, who refused to answer any questions during the investigation. Counsel to the Finance Committee to Re-elect the President and former FBI agent and Treasury official, Hunt was the planning director for the Bay of Pigs invasion and business partner of **Bernard Barker** in Nicaragua.

As a result of the Watergate fiasco, **Richard M. Nixon**, who had, himself, been a vigorous supporter of the Bay of Pigs invasion, was forced to resign the Presidency of the United States.

Richard M. Nixon &
Charles "Bebe" Rebozo

*Miami resident **Bebe Rebozo** was with ex-President **Richard Nixon** the night he decided to resign his presidency, which he did on August 8, 1974.*

May 1980 saw men behaving badly again in Miami when Miami's black community erupted in one of the worst race riots in our nation's history after several white policemen were acquitted in the brutal killing of black businessman **Arthur McDuffie**. Eighteen lives were lost in the riot and property damages topped $50 million.

The tables were turned, however, when black men committed atrocities against "the white devils" as members of the Nation of Yahweh which was based in Miami. Led by the self-proclaimed "God, son of God," **Yahweh Ben Yahweh** (who was born **Hulon Mitchell**), its followers are said to have murdered hundreds of white men, women and children, many of them "runaway teenage girls on drugs, hippies and the like, people who would not be missed when they disappeared."

Yahweh Ben Yahweh

Throughout the '80s, as Yahweh's organization grew, he amassed an incredible $100 million fortune and an empire of satellite temples, buildings, hotels, restaurants and retail stores spanning 22 states, as well as a fleet of white-painted cars, trucks and vans.

Yahweh became a cult hero in Miami, despite a beheading, a shooting murder, a mob killing, a public firebombing of an apartment complex and a series of grotesque murders wherein the victims' ears were cut off and taken back to Yahweh as war prizes.

Yet, for nearly a decade, Miami law enforcement looked the other way and white and black leaders alike sang his praises and embraced the new "black messiah." Incredibly, the Mayor of Miami, **Mayor Xavier Suarez,** even named October 7, 1990 "Yahweh Ben Yahweh Day."

A short time later, however, **Yahweh Ben Yahweh** and 15 of his followers were arrested and tried on federal racketeering charges in the death of 14 Miamians; prosecutors arguing that Yahweh had ordered his followers to kill for him.

Defended by former federal judge **Alcee Hastings,** Yahweh was acquitted of racketeering charges linking him to the murders and found guilty only on charges of conspiracy. Six of the others arrested were also found guilty of conspiracy, and the other nine were set free.

 *Although he was impeached and removed from his position as a United States District Court Judge, **Alcee Hastings** cleared his name and ran for office in Florida. He was elected to the House of Representatives in 1992, a position which he still holds, and diligently represents Dade, Broward, Palm Beach, Hendry, Martin, St. Lucie and Okeechobee counties.*

On September 26, 2001, just 15 days after the September 11th attacks by terrorists in New York, Washington and Pennsylvania, **Yahweh Ben Yahweh** was released from prison. Even though he has been categorized by U.S. Intelligence as a "terrorist," and even though 11 of the 19 al-Qaeda hijackers that attacked our country on September 11, 2001 resided in South Florida and trained for their evil mission in our flight schools, including ring-leader **Mohamed Atta**, Yahweh now freely resides in North Miami-Dade.

Perhaps Miami's highest profile assassination was the July 15, 1997 murder of international designer **Gianni Versace,** who was gunned down on the steps of his Miami Beach home. The killer, **Andrew Cunanan,** who was suspected of four other murders, committed suicide one week later while holed up in a houseboat less than two miles from the murder scene. Although the two homosexuals had met before, Cunanan's motive was never ascertained.

Today, Miami's most notorious bad boy resident is disgraced NFL jock, **O.J. Simpson**, who some say settled in South Dade because of Florida's liberal debtor laws.

Brazen bad girl, hotel heiress **Paris Hilton** also recently got sand in her shoes.

Gianni Versace

Mohamed Atta

"Not even the dead are safe in Miami."
- O.J. Simpson

That's Entertainment

From 1940 to the early 1960s, the hottest spot in Miami Beach was **Lou Walters'** world-famous *Latin Quarter* nightclub, which was modeled somewhat after the *Moulin Rouge* in Paris.

Located on Palm Island Drive, Walters and his partner **E.M. Loew,** owner of the *Loew's Theatres* empire, combined the world's most beautiful dancers, spectacular costumes and incredible sets with the era's biggest stars; **Frank Sinatra, Dean Martin** and **Jerry Lewis, Tony Bennett, Jack Benny,** and **Zsa Zsa Gabor.**

Surrounded by celebrities throughout her life, daughter **Barbara Walters**, who was schooled in Miami, would break into "the man's world of television journalism" and become one of the foremost journalists of our time.

Barbara Walters

From Egyptian President **Anwar Sadat,** to England's **Princess Diana,** to **Hillary Clinton** and **Monica Lewinsky,** Barbara has brought the world's most topical personalities into our living rooms.

Of special interest to Miamians were her two interviews with Cuban Dictator **Fidel Castro** (25 years apart), and her interview with **Juan Miguel Gonzalez,** the father of young Cuban refugee **Elian Gonzalez,** who captured America's heart when he was rescued from a capsized boat off Miami's shores on Thanksgiving Day 1999.

But before Barbara, there was Lou - and for nearly two decades, Miami Beach sizzled.

Jackie Gleason

"And away we go!" chimed **Jackie Gleason** accompanied by his familiar *one-two-skidoo* shuffle – and away we went – every Sunday night between 1964 and 1969, when 40 million viewers turned on their television sets and were transported to "the sun and fun capital of the world," Miami Beach. And, "how sweet it was."

Just four years earlier, **Elvis** swiveled into town for his first TV appearance after his Army discharge. Taped at the Fontainebleau Hotel, **Elvis** sang two duets with the legendary **Frank Sinatra**; Elvis's hit, *"Love Me Tender,"* and Sinatra's trademark, *"Witchcraft."*

But the "really, really big shew" was an **Ed Sullivan** show in February 1964, when he hosted **The Beatles** in a spot broadcast from the Deauville Hotel in Miami Beach. As guests of sofa tycoon **Bernard Castro, The Beatles** stayed in Miami for four days, frolicking on the beach, cruising Biscayne Bay on Castro's yacht, and frequenting Miami Beach's late-night hot spots. Thousands of screaming fans (mostly female) flooded the beach, and Beatlemania rocked Miami and the world.

The Beatles in Miami Beach

It's hard to believe anyone could rip the headlines away from **The Beatles** here on their first American tour, but a sports legend did.

Cassius Clay, aka **Muhammed Ali,** was training in Miami Beach for his bout against **Sonny Liston** when the "Fab Four" came to town. In an internationally publicized media extravaganza, all four Beatles – and a horde of reporters and photographers - went down to the world-famous Fifth Street Gym to meet Clay.

Much to Paul's annoyance, in an effort to steal the spotlight, Clay kept everyone waiting for 18 minutes before he made his entrance. But then it was all fun and games as the five of them clowned around, Clay even lifting Ringo in the air and declaring, "When Liston reads about **The Beatles** visiting me, he'll get so mad I'll knock him out in three." **The Beatles** were skeptical, especially George.

But, on February 25, 1964, Clay knocked Liston out in the 7th round becoming the new World Heavyweight Champ. He immediately announced his acceptance of the Islamic faith and his new identity as **Muhammed Ali,** keeping his name, his controversial religious beliefs and Miami Beach in the headlines for weeks.

When **The Beatles** were asked about Clay in a BBC interview upon their return to England, Paul, John and Ringo agreed, "He's a big lad," Ringo stating, "He's bigger than all of us put together." He's "the greatest." Just ask him.

Of Miami, **The Beatles** had nothing but praise, George stating, "I think I enjoyed the sun in Miami the most of all," and Ringo confirming, "I just loved all of it, you know. Especially Miami – the sun. I didn't even know what it meant till I went over there."

The Beatles with Cassius Clay

With sand firmly lodged in their shoes, **The Beatles** would return to Miami many times, often staying in The Grove with their friend **Rocky Williams,** for whom their classic tune *Rocky Raccoon* was penned and visiting with other friends who lived on North Bay Road.

A "really, really big shew" of another kind was given by rock star **Jim Morrison**, lead singer of **The Doors** in 1969, when he exposed himself on stage during a concert at Dinner Key. Arrested, Morrison was found guilty of exposure and profanity charges in 1970. His sentence was up on appeal when he died in Paris in 1971.

Although the detective series "Surfside 6" which was filmed in Indian Creek hit the airwaves in 1960, as well as the world premier of "Where the Boys Are" based in Fort Lauderdale, and the popular "Flipper" television series from 1964 to 1967 brought Miami Beach into America's living rooms, nothing that came before or after could compare to the impact of another weekly television series that exploded on the scene in 1984, **"Miami Vice."**

As pastel clad narcotics detectives, heartthrobs **Don Johnson** and **Philip Michael Thomas** tooled around town in a Ferrari Testarossa exposing Miami Beach's seedier side amidst a lush subtropical background, million dollar yachts and a bustling nightlife filled with intrigue and glamour.

Overnight, Miami Beach became the place to see and be seen. It became a showplace of fashion and trendiness as celebrities and photographers flocked to the city, but Miami would forever after be associated as much with glamour as it is with the international drug trade.

Don Johnson and Philip Michael Thomas

Since the 1930s when **Albert Warner** (Warner Bros.) and **Nicholas Schenck** (Metro-Goldwyn-Mayer) bought "castles by the sea" in Miami, some of entertainment's biggest stars have called Greater Miami and the Beaches their home, including **Sophia Loren**, **Madonna**, **Gloria Estefan**, **Julio** and **Enrique Iglesias**, **Sylvester Stallone**, **Jennifer Lopez**, **David Caruso** and long-time North Miami Beach residents, **The Bee Gees**.

Stars like these continue to keep Miami in the limelight and in the spotlight.

"Shoot for the moon. Even if you miss, you'll land among the stars."
- Les Brown

*The "Surfside 6" houseboat became one of commentator **Larry King's** venues.*

***Don Johnson** and **Philip Michael Thomas** were dinner guests of President **Ronald Reagan** at the White House on December 10, 1985.*

Good Sports

In 1965, with the help of Miami Mayor **Robert King High** and the availability of the Orange Bowl, Minneapolis lawyer **Joseph Robbie** partnered with "Make Room for Daddy" television star **Danny Thomas** and the Miami Dolphins was born. By 1969, Robbie had purchased Thomas's interest and became the majority owner of the team which included early NFL greats **Larry Csonka** and **Bob Griese**.

Bob Griese

Larry Csonka

The next year, after coaching the Baltimore Colts for seven years, **Don Shula** became Vice President and Head Coach, following Coach **George Wilson** who had come to the Dolphins after eight years with the Detroit Lions. Just two short years later, Shula would lead the Dolphins through a "perfect season," culminating in two consecutive Super Bowl wins; defeating Washington in the 1972-73 season and Minnesota the following year.

It would be nine years before the Dolphins would win their next playoff game.

Enter quarterback **Dan Marino**.

Dan Marino

In 1984, Robbie announced plans to build a multi-purpose stadium in north Dade County and August 16, 1987 marked the Dolphin's 22nd anniversary with the first game played in Joe Robbie Stadium against the Chicago Bears. Having been the only NFL team to beat the Bears in the 1985 season, they lost this pre-season game, 10 to 3.

Don Shula

Jimmy Johnson

Don Shula *lives on Indian Creek Island off Miami Beach.*

On January 7, 1990, **Joseph Robbie** died of respiratory failure at age 73 and the corporation was realigned to ensure continued administration by the Robbie family. Two months later, **H. Wayne Huizenga, Jr.**, Chairman of the Board and Chief Executive Officer of Blockbuster Video, purchased 50% of the Robbie Stadium Corporation and a 15% partnership in the Miami Dolphins.

In February 1992, the Dolphins acquired **"Mean" Joe Green**.

Don Shula continued as coach and, in 1993, was named "Sports Illustrated Sportsman of the Year;" the only professional coach ever to receive this honor.

Joseph Robbie

By 1994, Huizenga purchased the Robbies' remaining interests and became 100% owner of both the Dolphins and the Stadium. Three weeks later, he entered into an agreement with Shula which gave Shula an ownership interest in the team, in addition to retaining his Vice President/Head Coach status.

In January 1996, Shula, "the winningest coach in NFL history," retired and was succeeded by the club's Executive Vice President and General Manager, **Jimmy Johnson**. Later that year, the Stadium would enter into an agreement with Pro Player, the sports apparel division of Fruit of the Loom, and was renamed *Pro Player Park*.

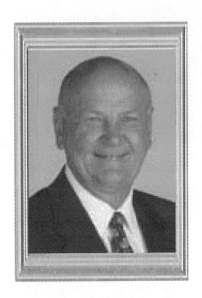

H. Wayne Huizenga, Jr.

Marino, the most prolific quarterback in NFL history, retired from professional football in 2000, after 16 years. However, he remains one of Miami's most beloved VIPs, founding the Dan Marino Foundation to raise money for various children's charities in South Florida with his wife Claire in 1995, and The Dan Marino Center, a comprehensive medical center for children with special needs, in 1998.

Like **Don Shula**, Marino is also a restaurant entrepreneur. Shula owns the world-famous *Shula's Steak House* in Miami Lakes and *Shula's on the Beach* in Ft. Lauderdale and Key West, plus 20 more restaurants nationwide and in Panama, and Dan owns the *Dan Marino's Town Tavern* chain of restaurants in South Florida.

Interestingly, **Dan Marino** was also an excellent baseball player. An exceptional pitcher, he was drafted after his senior year in high school in 1979 by the Kansas City Royals. Were it not for his dream of becoming a pro football player and his less than stellar academic performance his senior year, Miami sports could have turned out very differently. He was the 27th pick in the first round of the 1983 draft.

Since the early 1900s, when the **Tatum Brothers** lured the Boston Braves baseball team down to Miami to hold their spring training, many Major League teams have called South Florida their spring home, including the Giants, Reds, Athletics, Yankees, Pirates, Cardinals, Mets and Orioles. But it wasn't until 1993 that professional baseball came to Miami – compliments of Blockbuster Entertainment billionaire, **H. Wayne Huizenga,** when he bought the Florida Marlins.

Four short years later, the Marlins would win the World Series against the Cleveland Indians.

Abner Doubleday, credited with inventing the game of baseball in Cooperstown, NY in 1839 (although history has debunked this claim), fought in the Third Seminole War in Florida in the late 1850s. While he didn't play baseball (actually he disliked outdoor sports), Doubleday, who was considered a competent mapmaker, oversaw the construction of South Florida's Old Military Trail which ran from Fort Dallas to the New River in 1857.

By the early 1910s, Minor League baseball clubs had sprung up all over South Florida, including the not-so-famous Miami Magicians in 1912, and the Miami Tourists after World War I.

By World War II, the Florida East Coast League included such teams as the Miami Wahoos, the Miami Beach Flamingos, the Fort Lauderdale Tarpons and the West Palm Beach Indians.

Abner Doubleday

 Abner Doubleday is credited with firing the first shot of the Civil War.

After the end of the war, **Jose Manuel Aleman,** a former Minister of Education in Cuba, built the 9,000 seat Miami Stadium in Miami's Allapattah area, which opened on August 31, 1949. Spring home of the Baltimore Orioles for many years and the keeper of the city's Cuban baseball spirit, the Miami Stadium, renamed the *Bobby Maduro Stadium,* was the springtime playground of such baseball greats as **Mickey Mantle, Ted Williams, Jackie Robinson, Yogi Berra** and **Satchel Paige.** With its moveable bleachers and curved metal roof, the stadium was heralded as "the finest stadium in the land."

Class B teams in the early '50s included the Miami Sun Sox and the Fort Lauderdale Lions (who wore shorts during the 1953 season).

The Marlins nickname was first used in 1956, when legendary promoter **Bill Veeck** was brought in to run the team and baseball moved to the Orange Bowl. Sadly, poor attendance and other financial problems caused the Triple-A franchise to move to San Juan, Puerto Rico after the 1960 season.

Mickey Mantle

Ted Williams

Bill Veeck

The Triple-A franchise made a brief reappearance in South Florida in 1979, with the Miami Amigos of the Inter-American League, but financial problems led to its demise after only a few short months.

From July 1979 until April 1993, the only professional baseball above the Class A level in South Florida was played during the spring.

Satchel Paige

Huizenga, who was also the owner of both the Miami Dolphins and the Florida Panthers hockey team, sold the Marlins to **John W. Henry** in January 1999, who, just two years later, sold the franchise to Montreal Expos owner and New York art dealer **Jeffrey Loria**. Simultaneously, Henry bought the Boston Red Sox. The Expos, "stripped of everything but the light fixtures" in the bad-faith three-way sale, "bit the dust."

Loria, of course, would then astound the world when, in 2003, his Marlins would win another World Series championship, with 72-year-old **Jack McKeon** as manager, against the favored New York Yankees.

Jeffrey Loria

Jack McKeon

Although coach **Doug McLean** had taken the Panthers all the way to the Stanley Cup in only four years, the fastest in the history of the sport, that same year Huizenga sold the Panthers to a group of eight primary investors led by **Alan P. Cohen**, CEO of generic Fort Lauderdale drug maker Andrx Corp., staying on as a ninth minority partner.

Pat Riley

Sports has also been very good to another Miami billionaire, Carnival Corp. CEO **Micky Arison**, owner of the Miami Heat. Under head coach **Pat Riley**, the Heat earned four Atlantic Division titles and turned out some of professional basketball's greatest stars, including **Rony Seikaly, Glen Rice, Tim Hardaway** and Miami's own **Alonzo Mourning**.

Tim Hardaway

Rony Seikaly

 *The Heat's newest high-profile recruit, **Shaquille O'Neal**, recently got sand in his Reeboks™; he bought **Rony Seikaly's** estate on Star Island.*

Mourning, although stricken with a serious kidney disorder that forced him off the court for awhile, like Dolphin's quarterback **Dan Marino** and NFL Hall of Famer **Nick Buoniconti** who founded the Miami Project to Cure Paralysis, devotes his time and energies to helping Miami's youngest citizens. His Overtown Youth Center, a venture of Alonzo Mourning Charities, Inc., located at 14th St. and 3rd Ave., provides everything from computers, art and music to bodybuilding and team sports. Privately financed by Miami developer **Martin Z. Margulies,** the Center is dedicated to improving the lives of Miami's most underprivileged children.

In 2003, after two disappointing seasons, **Pat Riley** resigned as head coach of the Heat, remaining team president, but passing the "ball" to his assistant of 8 years, **Stan Van Gundy.**

Alonzo Mourning

**Miami City Manager Carlos Jimenez,
Alonzo Mourning & Marty Margulies**

"Sports do not build character. They reveal it."
- Heywood Broun

The Ugly American

The "Ugly Award" goes to former beauty queen and American songbird, **Anita Bryant,** a long-time Miami resident who had a 33-room mansion on Biscayne Bay.

In 1977, the Metro-Dade Commission became the latest in a series of boards across the country to pass a gay rights ordinance, but within hours of the Commission passing the ordinance, the city experienced a phenomenon that had never occurred before nor since – it snowed in Miami.

Some took this as a sign from God.

Appalled by the ruling, Bryant, a devout Christian and patriot who entertained the troops with **Bob Hope** in Vietnam, began a passionate "Save Our Children" campaign against gay rights, designed to "save children from recruitment by homosexuals." She took her bigotry-laden crusade on the road and it was during this tour that the famous "pie-in-the-face" incident occurred at a televised news conference in Des Moines.

As the national spokesperson for Florida orange juice, the negative backlash from her campaign resulted in a boycott of Florida orange juice. When the controversy cut into growers' pockets and corporate profits, Anita lost her job.

Although she was able to persuade the voters of Dade County to overturn the ordinance, her attack on the homosexual community drew tens of thousands of new recruits to the "Gay Pride" movement, forever galvanizing the alternative lifestyle.

Bryant's marriage crumbled, she moved from Miami and faded into obscurity.

Anita Bryant

"We have just enough religion to make us hate, but not enough to make us love one another."
- Jonathan Swift

 Anita Bryant *was invited to the White House 14 times by President* **Lyndon Johnson** *and sang "The Battle Hymn of the Republic" and "God Bless America" at both the Democratic and Republican National Conventions.*

Colorful Characters

A lady lion tamer, a beloved public drunk, an eccentric billionaire and a man in love; these are just a few of the colorful characters that have called Greater Miami their home and given the city some of its colorful character.

Carl Fisher, the man who invented Miami Beach, was one of history's most colorful characters. Antics like riding a bicycle across a tightrope to sell bicycles and hoisting a car from a hot air balloon to sell automobiles were just some of the publicity stunts employed by the man who was a master of selling the "sizzle rather than the steak." Typical of his larger than life advertising gimmicks was the time he enlisted the aid of his pet elephant Rosie to act as golf caddie for president-elect **Warren G. Harding** on a visit to Miami in the early 1920s.

Rosie the Elephant with Golfer

Much to the dismay of **William Pruden Smith,** who was Mayor of Miami at the time, Fisher literally hijacked Harding away from Mayor Smith and Miami Chamber of Commerce President **E.G. Sewell**, and brought him to his newly built Flamingo Hotel on Miami Beach.

From then on, Fisher never left his side.

Knowing that Harding was an avid fisherman, Fisher employed the services of renowned fisherman **Captain Charlie Thompson** and took the president-elect on a two-day fishing expedition to The Cocolobo Club on the north bank of Caesar's Creek, completely monopolizing his time.

Overwhelmed by Fisher's razzle-dazzle and Captain Thompson's fishing prowess, after his brief stay Harding publicly endorsed the city to the press stating, "Because of the attractiveness of Miami and Miami Beach, I hope to come here again. This beach is wonderful. It is developing like magic."

Miami Beach had its first national dateline and the resulting publicity was priceless.

 Captain Charlie Thompson played host to four presidents, Grover Cleveland, Warren Harding, Teddy Roosevelt and Woodrow Wilson, and one time hooked a 30,000 pound whale shark that had a 3,000 pound fish in its belly.

A hard drinker, Fisher became drinking buddies with a former *Athletics* baseball player who had a reputation for being "one of baseball's dirtiest of players;" a man who publicly admitted to having a "weakness of character" and spent several overnight stays in the police drunk tank, **Louis F. Snedigear**.

After obtaining a law degree and spending a few years with the Miami law firm of *Shutts, Smith and Bowen*, Snedigear went into the real estate business and became fast friends with Fisher. Despite his bouts with the bottle (even though this was during Prohibition) and several automotive mishaps, the people loved him and elected him Mayor of Miami Beach – four times – more than any other mayor in the city's history.

Not nearly as public, but perhaps just as bizarre, was newspaper billionaire **William Randolph Hearst**. In 1925, he purchased the cloisters of an ancient Spanish monastery and had it completely dismantled and packed piece-by-piece in 11,000 crates which were carefully numbered and cataloged. Unfortunately, due to a hoof-and-mouth disease scare that swept the country at the time, upon arrival in Miami all the numbered crates were opened, the stones washed, the hay burned, and then everything was haphazardly repacked - where it would remain dormant for 26 years.

After Hearst's death in 1952, Miamians **Raymond Moss** and **William Edgemon** bought the monastery and had it meticulously reassembled. The task took a dozen years and cost almost $1.5 million.

Located on Dixie Highway in North Miami-Dade, the Ancient Spanish Monastery, originally built in 1141, is considered the "Oldest Building in America." Open to the public, the monastery continues to host a myriad of weddings, receptions and events.

William Randolph Hearst

 *Frank B. **Shutts**, head of the Shutts, Smith and Bowen law firm, was **Carl Fisher's** attorney and the founder of the "Miami Herald".*

Another unusual structure that is unique to Miami and the world was built by Latvian immigrant **Edward Leedskalnin**. Broken-hearted after his love, a girl named **Agnes Skuvst**, who he referred to as "Sweet Sixteen," left him standing at the alter, he roamed the country until, in 1918, he developed tuberculosis.

South Florida's climate drew him to a sparsely-settled section of Florida City which he chose to "get away from the world," attend to his health and nurse his broken heart. There, he would embark on a 20+ year odyssey wherein, working completely alone, only at night, and with unknown resources in complete secrecy, he would create a tribute to his "Sweet Sixteen," a curious collection of massive sculptures carved out of the area's native coral rock which he quarried on site. Among its mysteries are a nine-ton entrance gate, a tower which, alone, weighs 243 tons, a one-piece spiral staircase, a 25-foot high telescope, and a rocking chair that weighs thousands of pounds yet is so delicately balanced that it moves with a touch of a finger.

Also displayed is a crescent moon sculpted from a 30-ton rock flanked by Mars and a ringed Saturn, each the size of an automobile, but made out of solid rock. Several pieces are signed, "Ed."

In 1936, after a robbery attempt, Leedskalnin moved his sculptures to their current site in Homestead and, single-handedly, erected a wall to surround the property that measures eight-feet tall by four-feet wide by three-feet thick and weighs approximately 13,000 pounds. After all these years, the stones in the wall still butt together in a clean, tight fit, completely intact, despite having been constructed without cement.

All this, the 95-lb. Leedskalnin accomplished by himself, in the dark of night, using only simple hand tools. The secret of how he was able to move the huge coral rocks weighing up to 35 tons each was never discovered.

In 1984, Leedskalnin's Coral Castle, originally named Rock Gate Park, was placed on the National Register of Historic Places.

Edward Leedskalnin

 The Coral Castle is located at 28655 S. Dixie Hwy. (Public)

Julia Field

Another colorful character, **Julia Field,** the wife of anthropologist **Henry Field** (grand-nephew of department store chain founder and philanthropist **Marshall Field**), lived in the property known as "La Brisa" on Main Highway in Coconut Grove for nearly four decades.

In 1948, with three monkeys, one goat and two black bears, Julia started the Crandon Park Zoo, named for County Commissioner **Charles Crandon,** the "Father of Florida's far flung parks," who was also responsible for locating the world-famous Seaquarium on Virginia Key rather than near the Haulover inlet where it was originally planned.

Julia, an attractive lion tamer, was the zoo's curator.

Over the years, the zoo's collection grew to more than 1,200 animals, when Hurricane Betsy in 1965 put three feet of water over most of the area, causing the deaths of nearly 250 animals. Talks began about a new location and, when the Richmond Naval Air Station property became available in the early '70s, Dade County purchased 600 acres for a new zoo.

Construction began in 1975, and Miami's Metrozoo opened on July 4, 1980.

 Prior to **Julia Field,** "La Brisa's" former owner and resident was Miami pioneer and world-renown author, **Kirk Munroe.**

 Charles Crandon was also responsible for creating the Dade County Port Authority and the merger of Pan American Field with the Army Air Transport field, thus creating the present site of today's Miami International Airport.

In 1983, the nation and the rest of the world looked at Miami and the Beaches trough rose-colored glasses, when a bizarre yet wonderful Bulgarian artist, **Christo Javacheff ("Christo"),** conceived the idea of covering 11 islands in Biscayne Bay with pink plastic.

Six and a half million square feet of polypropylene and three million dollars later, the "Surrounded Islands" were complete and the color of Miami was unmistakably pink.

Viewed by millions via TV and satellite, Miami and the rest of the world smiled.

Christo Javacheff

"The distance between insanity and genius is measured only by success."
- **James Bond**: Tomorrow Never Dies

Mothers (and Fathers) of Invention

Over the years many famous inventors called South Florida their home including **Alexander Graham Bell** (inventor of the telephone among other accolades), whose daughter was married to horticulturist **David Fairchild**, for whom Fairchild Tropical Gardens is named.

So, too, **Thomas Edison**, who held more than 1,000 patents for his inventions, spent a great many years basking in Florida's sunshine, settling in the Fort Myers area. Great friends, Bell and Edison worked together to perfect the phonograph.

Alexander Graham Bell

David Grandison Fairchild

 *When the Miami Telephone Company went to **Alexander Graham Bell's** house to install a telephone for him, he refused, stating that he "seldom used the instrument as it intruded upon the privacy of others."*

Another good friend of Bell, aviator **Glenn Curtiss** was also an extremely prolific inventor, not only inventing several airplane engines and hydroaeroplanes (planes that could take off and land on water), but also wing flaps, retractable landing gear and the enclosed cockpit. Plus, he invented the world's fastest motorcycle, the motorcycle handlebar throttle control and the world's first airboat.

Bitter rival of the **Wright Brothers,** Curtiss spent several years locked in patent litigation with the two brothers, resulting in the Wrights filing nearly three dozen lawsuits against Curtiss and others. In the end, however, while Curtiss made better airplanes, **Orville Wright** won in court (**Wilbur** having died of typhoid fever before the litigation was complete).

Some lesser known inventors: Miami resident **Rose O'Neill** invented the world-famous Kewpie Doll in 1913; **Arthur Wynne,** a New Jersey transplant, invented the crossword puzzle as a means of entertainment for his children in 1920; and **Robert Cade** invented both the hydraulic football helmet and the refreshing sport drink "Gatorade" in the mid-1960s.

Life-altering for all Miamians as well as the rest of the world, the inventor of air-conditioning, **John Gorrie,** was also a Floridian.

Glenn Curtiss

Rose O'Neill

Glenn Curtiss is credited with being "the first to make a public flight in the United States, the first to sell a commercial airplane, the first to fly from one American city to another, and the first to receive a U.S. pilot license," Pilot License #1. An avid archery fan, Curtiss also invented the short-lived game of Archery Golf.

Another great inventor who is honored alongside **Benjamin Franklin** and **Thomas Edison** in both the Business Hall of Fame and the National Inventors' Hall of Fame, was a Belgian-born scientist who lived on Biscayne Bay at the turn of the 20th century and invented a material that changed "the stuff our world is made of."

Leo Baekeland, in search of a non-flammable substance to serve as an insulator for the burgeoning electrical and automotive industries, discovered a material that would not melt yet could be molded, resisted most acids, and could be dyed bright colors. The material, which he called "Bakelite," was the predecessor of today's plastic.

Leo Baekeland

Already a millionaire from the sale of his first invention, Velox, a photographic paper which he sold to the *George Eastman and Kodak Company* in 1899, Bakelite afforded Baekeland international recognition and fame. When he retired in 1939, he sold his successful plastics company to Union Carbide and Carbon Corporation, bequeathing his enormous wealth to his progeny.

In an ironic twist of fate, his great-grandson **Tony Baekeland,** while serving a prison sentence for stabbing his mother to death in 1972, committed suicide -- by suffocating himself with a plastic bag tied tightly around his neck.

"Genius is 1% inspiration and 99% perspiration."
- **Thomas Alva Edison**

Leo Baekeland is said to have been such a genius that his brain is kept in the Smithsonian.

Bakelite was the first Western industry to be established in Japan. Today, products that were made with Bakelite are highly collectible.

Politically Incorrect

"The bigger they come, the harder they fall." No other statement rings as true when it comes to our elected officials who, through greed or malice, have fallen from their thrones and landed, in many cases, behind bars.

In 1991, two-time Miami Mayor **Alex Daoud** was indicted on 41 counts of extortion. Since then, dozens of Miami politicians have followed in his footsteps and succumbed to temptation.

On one of **Dr. Paul George's** famous historical tours highlighting the "murder, mystery and mayhem" in Miami, we drove by Miami's City Hall and cruised through the parking lot. Each parking space had a Miami politician's name imprinted on its curb stop. Dr. George glibly named off one politician after another, many with addendums of "indicted for..." or "currently in prison for...."

His dissertation would have been amusing, if it were not for the shear number of those indicted.

Alex Daoud

 *Miami Mayor **Alex Daoud** once appeared as a reporter on the television series Mission: Impossible (1968) and as a judge on an episode of Miami Vice (1989).*

A few examples:

Cesar Odio, the first City Manager in Miami's history to be indicted for corruption in plotting a kickback scheme with the City of Miami's health insurance program;

Miami City Commissioner **Miller Dawkins,** also convicted of corruption charges for soliciting a $100,000 kickback from mainframe computer-maker Unisys in exchange for $20 million in city contracts; and

Miami's second City Manager, Ex-Police Chief **Donald Warshaw,** whose troubles began with his association with accountant **Ronald Stern** and an embezzling scheme which took a total of $1.3 million dollars from both the Miami Police Relief Pension Fund and a city-funded program called "Do the Right Thing," established to recognize youngsters for outstanding deeds. $800,000 was paid back, but Warshaw's problems escalated when Mayor **Joe Carollo** fired him for refusing to fire Police Chief **William O'Brien** when he failed to inform Carollo of the impending federal raid on the home of **Elian Gonzalez's** relatives in April 2000. The ensuing circus of "dueling news conferences" and name-calling between Warshaw and Carollo was a national embarrassment.

Donald Warshaw

William O'Brien

Joe Carollo

Warshaw's woes culminated with his imprisonment in 2001 on charges of corruption and mail fraud stemming from his earlier involvement with the "Do the Right Thing" program and police pension fund. He was ordered to pay a $30,000 fine, plus complete restitution for the money he stole in addition to serving one year plus one day in prison.

*Accountant **Ronald Stern, Donald Warshaw's** associate, committed suicide in 1999.*

Other Miami officials indicted include: Commissioner and Vice Mayor of Miami, **Demetrio Perez, Jr.**, who was indicted for pocketing $1 million from money earmarked for at-risk children; and

Demetrio Perez, Jr.

Humberto Hernandez

Commissioner **Humberto Hernandez**, who was indicted twice, first on federal bank fraud and money laundering charges, for which he was found guilty, and then for his involvement in "fixing" the 1997 Miami mayoral election which put ex-Miami Mayor **Xavier Suarez** back in office – albeit for only four months – until the election was overturned and **"Crazy Joe" Carollo** was reinstated as Mayor.

While Suarez was never officially charged or found guilty of any personal involvement in the massive absentee-ballot vote fraud scheme, Hernandez was found guilty of the charges and sent to prison along with his chief financial aide and a dozen other city officials.

Interestingly, the same man who prosecuted Hernandez, **Bruce Udolf**, the chief federal prosecutor for public corruption in South Florida, also won a conviction against Hialeah Mayor **Raul Martinez** on extortion and racketeering charges, but a federal court was forced to overturn the case when two hung juries failed to convict. Forced to step down, not only was Martinez re-elected to office, he also collected $1.2 million in back pay!

Xavier Suarez

*Esther Ortiz, ex-wife of former Miami Commissioner **Humberto Hernandez**, married the lawyer who represented Hernandez at his vote fraud trial in April 2003; an affair which began during the trial – which Hernandez lost.*

South Florida has been involved in other election shenanigans over the years, as the 2000 Bush-Gore Presidential election will attest to.

In 2000, the entire world waited two long months, through recount after recount, as the state of Florida was put under a microscope. Ballots were meticulously scrutinized and accusations of voter irregularities flew between both parties. After prematurely declaring **Al Gore** the winner on election night, in the end, Florida's 25 electoral votes and the Presidency of the United States went to **George W. Bush**.

Al Gore

George W. Bush

 *In the 2000 Presidential election, ex-Mayor **Xavier Suarez**, a member of the executive committee of the Miami-Dade Republican Party, "helped fill out absentee ballot forms and enlist Republican absentee voters in Miami-Dade County," despite his questionable vote fraud history.*

This was not the first time, however, that a Presidential election was held up by the State of Florida.

In 1876, the outcome of the election between Republican Governor **Rutherford B. Hayes** of Ohio and Democrat **Samuel J. Tilden,** Governor of New York, was held up for four months, dependent upon contested electoral votes in Oregon, Louisiana, South Carolina and Florida. With Hayes' 165 electoral votes to Tilden's 184, Hayes needed all four states (20 electoral votes) in order to win the Presidency.

The election in Florida was at a tie, dependent upon the tally in Dade County comprised of only 28 votes. As the nation waited, the *Louisville Courier Journal* ran the memorable headline, "Where the Hell is Dade County?"

Rutherford B. Hayes

Dade County's votes were in the hands of the ex-lieutenant governor and self-proclaimed "King of Dade," Republican Carpetbagger **William H. Gleason.**

William H. Gleason

With a history of "fixing" several Florida elections to his favor, Gleason, unhappy with the County's results, decided to personally deliver the votes to Tallahassee rather than mail them.

He took the long way.

By the time he reached Tallahassee six weeks later, the Senate and House Special Committees had formed a bi-partisan Electoral Commission, independent of Congress, for the sole purpose of adjudication in disputed electoral returns.

Comprised of eight Republicans and seven Democrats, Republican Hayes won all contests by an 8 to 7 vote. With 185 electoral votes to Tilden's 184, the Presidency of the United States went to **Rutherford B. Hayes.**

Although he honorably served in office with honesty and integrity healing many of the wounds caused by Reconstruction, because he had allegedly stolen the election, Hayes was nicknamed "His Fraudulency," a legacy that unfortunately remains.

"Vote early and vote often."
- Al Capone

Outstanding Individuals

Marjory Stoneman Douglas
"The Defender of the Everglades"

The Written Word

Nineteenth century novelist **Benjamin Disraeli** (who was England's first and only Jewish Prime Minister) once wrote, "The best way to become acquainted with a subject is to write about it."

Fortunately, many Miami historians, journalists and authors have felt the same way and, throughout history, were able to capture Miami's essence and eloquently transfer it to the written word.

The first European to travel through Florida and write about it was **Hernando Escalante d'Fontaneda,** a white man who was shipwrecked and taken captive by the Tequesta Indians in 1549. In his memoirs published in 1575, he described Miami as, "...situated on the bank of a river which extends into the country the distance of 15 leagues, and issues from another lake of fresh water, which is said by some Indians who have traveled it more than I, to be an arm of the Lake of Mayaimi [Lake Okeechobee]."

It would be almost 300 years before the name "Miami" would appear in print again.

In May of 1896, even before Miami was incorporated as a city, it had a newspaper, the *Miami Metropolis*. Funded by **Henry Flagler,** its first editor was **Dr. Walter S. Graham,** a physician and lawyer for Flagler's railroad. Contributors to the paper were some of Miami's earliest pioneers.

Dr. Walter S. Graham

Decades later another journalist, **Howard Kleinberg** (who was editor of the now-defunct *Miami News* for many years) incorporated many of these original articles into a wonderful book called, "Miami. The way we were."

Howard Kleinberg

Another Kleinberg book simply titled, "Miami Beach," paired Kleinberg with beloved Miami historian and author, **Arva Moore Parks,** who also penned the official history of Miami, "Miami: The Magic City," as well as numerous other books, articles and films.

Howard Kleinberg continues to write and his son, **Eliot Kleinberg,** has also authored several books on Miami, though quite different from those written by his father.

Arva Moore Parks

Other notable historians include Coral Gables resident **Charleton W. Tebeau**, author of the 1971 book, "A History of Florida," the first definitive chronological text on Florida's past, author and long-time journalist for the *Sun-Sentinel*, **Stuart McIver**, and **Dr. Thelma Peters**; extraordinary people who wrote about extraordinary times.

Charleton Tebeau

In 1994, Miami developer **Ralph Bodek** presented Florida's colorful past in a whole new way, with his "painless, informative and revealing" book, "Miami Poppycock;" a truly enjoyable read.

Ralph Bodek

Today, Miami's own resident historian, **Dr. Paul George**, teacher, prolific author, tour guide and friend, continues to unearth exciting new details about Miami's past and keeps Miami's history alive with his books, articles, classes at Miami-Dade Community College and tours sponsored by the Historical Association of Southern Florida. A favorite of interviewers, rarely a week goes by that Dr. George cannot be seen on local television, in the newspaper or leading a crusade to save one of Miami's historical treasures.

Dr. Paul George

 Charleton Tebeau was one of the founders of the Historical Museum of Southern Florida.

Ralph Bodek was one of the developers of Miami's 163rd Street Shopping Center.

Tennessee Williams

Many famous writers of fiction have also called Greater Miami and the Beaches their home, including **Zane Grey, Ernest Hemingway** and **Tennessee Williams**.

James Whitcomb Riley, aka "The Hoosier Poet," wintered in Miami Beach and **Robert Frost** "took the road less traveled by" which led him to Coconut Grove - he spent his winters there in the 1940s and '50s.

Robert Frost

The Grove was also home to cartoonist **Don Martin** of *Mad Magazine* fame.

"History shall be kind to me for I shall write it."
      - Sir Winston Churchill

Local Heroes

"Champions are made from something they have deep inside them: A desire, a dream a vision..."

Muhammad Ali was speaking of a "champion" in terms of excelling in sports when he uttered those words, but the same can be said of a "champion" in terms of a cause or purpose. Miami is fortunate to have had many such "champions;" men and women who have come to the aid of the people, the environment and social and economic causes.

Probably Miami's greatest local hero was **Henry Flagler**. Nicknamed "the Benevolent Dictator" by author **Arva Moore Parks**, not only did Flagler bring his railroad to Miami and with it civilization, he also personally bought and paid for the lumber that built the city, the electricity that drove it, the streets that paved it and the food that fed the men and women in his employ. In addition, Flagler built the city's first two hospitals and donated the building and books for Miami's first library.

Henry Morrison Flagler

After the 1926 hurricane and the stock market crash of 1929, it was **Alfred I. duPont** who came to the rescue of Florida's floundering banks. A substantial investor in Miami real estate, when duPont died, he placed his considerable fortune into a Trust, The Nemours Foundation, which continues to benefit children and seniors throughout the world.

Alfred I. duPont

 *A prolific inventor, **Alfred duPont** was awarded more than 200 patents for his inventions.*

Seniors were fortunate to have an advocate of another kind in **Claude Denson Pepper** who represented Florida in the U.S. Congress for almost 27 years. Pepper became a national champion of civil rights and of the government's responsibility to our nation's elderly.

He abolished age discrimination in the workplace, strengthened the Medicare program and assured seniors a decent retirement income with the Social Security program. He also sponsored bills supporting National Health Care, cancer and heart disease research programs, a minimum wage and equal pay for equal work for women.

Claude Denson Pepper

Diogenes once said, *"The foundation of every state is the education of its youth."* Toward that end, Florida's children found their champion in **Napoleon Bonaparte Broward** (a one-time gunrunner during the Spanish-American War), for whom Broward County is named.

As Florida's 19th governor from 1905 to 1909, he passed several education bills which raised qualifications and increased pay for teachers, adopted a uniform system of textbooks and codification of school laws, rules and regulations, enacted Florida's first compulsory school education and school attendance laws, and placed restrictions on child labor laws. On May 29, 1907, he signed a bill which prohibited "the employment of minors under a certain age in factories, workshops, bowling alleys, barrooms, beer gardens, places of amusement where intoxicating liquors are sold, and in or about mine or quarry…" He also unified the state's higher learning institutions under a board of control.

Broward was also a champion of the environment, enacting several conservation laws protecting fish, oysters, game and Florida's forests. In fact, Broward always maintained his chief interest throughout his administration was to "save and reclaim the people's land" and actually led the first campaign to successfully drain and develop portions of the Everglades.

Napoleon Bonaparte Broward

 Napoleon Broward had nine children.

One cannot speak of the Everglades without mentioning the Everglades' greatest champion, **Marjory Stoneman Douglas**, Miami's resident local hero for almost 85 years. However, unlike **Napoleon Broward**, Douglas spent the last 40 years of her life fighting *against* development in the Everglades. In fact, in 1969, she helped found the Friends of the Everglades, an educational advisory group dedicated to the protection and restoration of the Everglades' ecosystem.

An independent thinker and passionate orator, Douglas is best known for her book, *The Everglades: River of Grass,* first published in 1947. A "tough old woman," Marjory lived in the same Coconut Grove home from 1924 until her death at age 108 in 1998.

Marjory Stoneman Douglas

 *In 1993, **Marjory Stoneman Douglas** was awarded the Presidential Medal of Honor by President **Bill Clinton**.*

The Everglades had another champion in lawyer **Spessard Lindsey Holland**. He was instrumental in creating both the Everglades National Park and the Florida Game and Fresh Water Commission.

Holland served as governor during World War II and spent 24 years as a senator, serving under five Presidents; Truman, Eisenhower, Kennedy, Johnson and Nixon.

Spessard Lindsey Holland

 *An elected Polk County judge in 1920, eight years later **Spessard Holland** returned to private practice and formed a partnership that would evolve into the international law firm of Holland & Knight.*

Miami Beach's "environment" found its local hero in writer **Barbara Baer Capitman** who looked at the buildings on South Beach (mostly built in the 1930s and '40s) and saw a treasure instead of an eyesore. In an effort to save this piece of Miami's history, Capitman and her dear friend, industrial designer **Leonard Horowitz,** would found the Miami Design Preservation League in 1976.

By adding a splash of pastel color to what had previously been whitewashed edifices and resurrecting the chipped Art Deco hotel facades to their original glory, crowds returned to Miami Beach as visitors – and investors.

In 1979, Miami Beach's Art Deco District (approximately one square mile in diameter) was placed on the National Register of Historic Places.

Barbara Baer Capitman

 The Art Deco District is the only development listed in the National Register of Historic Places that is comprised entirely of 20th Century buildings.

Women found their champion in **Roxcy O'Neal Bolton**, another long-time local resident who spent three decades championing the plight of abused women, domestic violence and discrimination in the workplace. In 1966, she helped form the National Organization for Women.

In 1969, she successfully challenged the practice that many restaurants had of keeping a separate "men only" section, eliciting a public statement from *Burdine's* conceding that they "...made the decision to change the name, and the "men only" concept, as expeditiously as possible."

Bolton also founded the Miami-based Women in Distress shelters for abused women and was instrumental in establishing the Rape Treatment Center, the first of its kind, at Jackson Memorial Hospital in 1974. The Rape Treatment Center was re-named in **Roxcy Bolton's** honor in 1993.

Roxcy Bolton

*The Women's Park, located at 10251 W. Flagler Street in Miami, a dream of pioneer feminist **Roxcy Bolton**, contains a time capsule with mementos of outstanding Florida women, including **Marjory Stoneman Douglas**, African-American author **Zora Neale Hurston** and Cuban anthropologist **Lydia Cabrera**. The capsule is scheduled to be opened on August 26, 2020, the centennial of the Woman Suffrage Amendment.*

Bryan Norcross

August 24, 1992 brought Miami a real-life action hero, **Bryan Norcross**, the meteorologist who tirelessly "talked South Florida through" Hurricane Andrew. Norcross saved many lives that night with his sound advice, calmly delivered from what appeared to be a closet deep within the bowels of WTVJ Channel 6.

Bryan's three-day vigil began Saturday night, two days before Andrew struck land, and when he told viewers to "Get out, get out now," most did.

Unfortunately, many of those who left the beach to move inland ran directly into danger when Andrew shifted and slammed into Kendall. Norcross's sage advice to "Go into your closets," "Get into the bathtub or a closet, pull a mattress over you and your loved ones," saved thousands of people whose houses were torn apart by the ferocious 168 mph winds.

With damages totaling $30 billion, Hurricane Andrew was the single most costly natural disaster in American history. Thanks to **Bryan Norcross**, it was not the most costly in terms of the number of lives it took; 4 in the Bahamas, 8 in Louisiana, and 11 from Dade County.

A Miami Beach resident for most of his life, Bryan received the 1993 David Brinkley Award for Excellence in Communication, is the recipient of an Emmy Award from the Suncoast Chapter of the National Association of Arts and Sciences, and has received both the DuPont and Peabody awards, broadcasting's highest honors.

He's our hero.

"Show me a hero and I will write you a tragedy."
        - F. Scott Fitzgerald

Black and White

Although there were many "separatists" after the Civil War, segregation did not become a major issue in Miami until well into the 1900s, when builders began discriminating against both blacks and Jews.

Even before Miami was incorporated as a city, blacks, mostly from the nearby Bahamian islands, settled in significant numbers in Coconut Grove. Since 1784, when England traded Florida to Spain in order to acquire the Bahamas, these black pioneers worked side-by-side with Miami's earliest white pioneers, carving a home out of the wilderness.

In 1897, **E.W.F. Stirrup,** a black man, owned most of what is today's downtown Coconut Grove, including the Charlotte Jane Memorial Park Cemetery on Charles Avenue and Douglas Road (a historical treasure worth strolling through).

In addition, when **Henry Flagler's** railroad arrived in 1896, he brought with him hundreds of disenfranchised black laborers who came first to build the railroad and then to build his Royal Palm Hotel. Of the 344 voters who incorporated Miami as a city, more than one-third were blacks recruited from Flagler's entourage. In fact, the very first registered voter was **Silos Austin**, a black man, and the first person to sign the city charter was **W.H. Artson,** another black man; a tailor who worked for Flagler. Many of these laborers settled in "Colored Town," today's Overtown.

12 Black Laborers from Flagler's Crew
Breaking Ground for Flagler's Royal Palm Hotel
A.W. Brown, Philip Bowman, Jim Hawkins, Warren Merridy, Richard Mangrom, Romeo Fashaw, Scipio Coleman, Sim Anderson, David Heartly, J.B. Brown, William Collier and Joe Thompson

 *Stirrup's granddaughter, **Dr. Dazelle Dean Simpson,** who grew up in her grandfather's Coconut Grove home, became Florida's first board-certified Black pediatrician, practicing in Overtown and Liberty City for more than 40 years before retiring.*

In 1900, the U.S. Census showed 966 blacks living in Miami, not including Coconut Grove's Bahamian community, and by 1910, that number grew to 2,258, nearly 50% of Miami's 5,500 populous.

In 1913, attorney **R.E.S. Toomey** opened Miami's first African-American law practice and was responsible for organizing voter registration efforts as early as 1920.

In 1914, **Kelsey Pharr,** an educated black man from Salisbury, North Carolina, came to Miami to work as a bellhop and waiter at **Henry Flagler's** Royal Palm Hotel in order to raise money to finish medical school.

While in Flagler's employ, the city's black undertaker died and Pharr, along with three silent partners (also waiters at the Royal Palm Hotel) took over the undertaking business with Pharr providing embalming services and the others providing the initial capital.

Within three years, Pharr bought out his partners and, in 1937, purchased the Lincoln Memorial Park Cemetery from **F.B. Miller,** a white realtor.

Lincoln Memorial Park Cemetery became the city's first black cemetery and is the final resting place of many of Miami's black pioneers, including Pharr, **John Culmer, D.A. Dorsey** and **H.E.S. Reeves,** founder of the now-defunct *Miami Times*, the country's oldest black-owned newspaper, which began publication in 1923.

Dr. Kelsey Pharr

Dana Albert Dorsey, Miami's first black millionaire, started as a carpenter and amassed his fortune by buying land, building houses and renting them to blacks. As one of black Miami's greatest benefactors, Dorsey donated land for the black community's first library, high school and park, and was trustee for Miami's first black hospital, Christian Hospital, which was founded by Miami's first black physician, **Dr. William Sawyer.**

The former owner of Fisher Island (then called Terminal Island), Dorsey intended to develop the island as a resort community for wealthy blacks. However, with too many obstacles to overcome, Dorsey would sell the island to entrepreneur **Carl Fisher,** the maker of Miami Beach, a short time after he purchased it in 1918.

Liberty City was first developed in the 1920s by white developer **Floyd Davis,** who purchased the land from black families and hired a black salesman, **Alonzo Kelly,** to re-sell the lots to other blacks.

Dana Albert Dorsey

 D.A. Dorsey was the alternate delegate to the Republican National Convention from Florida in 1920.

Dr. William Sawyer's daughter, Gwen Cherry, became the first black woman to be elected to the State Legislature; an office she held for four terms before her accidental death in a car crash.

Fisher Island, today the richest real estate per capita in the nation, sold for $1 per acre in the early 1890s.

Concerned with the number of tuberculosis deaths in Liberty City, **Father John Culmer,** an Episcopalian priest, began a crusade to improve sanitary conditions in the community. Finally, in 1937, the federal government developed Liberty Square, Miami's first public housing project, complete with concrete structures and indoor plumbing, and a mass exodus ensued from Overtown to this new, modern community located at NW 62nd St. and 12th Ave.

Sadly, a five-foot tall wall was erected on the eastern boundary of Liberty Square, stretching along NW 12th Ave. from 62nd St. to 71st St., separating the black community from the white community. Although torn down in the 1950s, remnants of "The Wall" remain standing; a poignant reminder of previous racial attitudes.

In 1991, ex-President **Jimmy Carter** helped build 14 low-income homes in Liberty City as a volunteer worker for Habitat for Humanity.

Jimmy Carter

Another early black community, Lemon City, a farming community with a natural deepwater channel, at 61st and Lemon Ave., boasted the area's largest population at the time of Miami's incorporation. Originally named "Motto" in honor of **Chief Motto,** a Seminole Indian Chief, it was renamed in 1882 because of the abundance of lemon trees that grew in the area.

Dr. John Dupuis, a dairy farmer and owner of the White Belt Dairy, founded the city, comprised mostly of blacks from the Caribbean. Absorbed into Greater Miami in 1925, Lemon City was almost completely destroyed in 1960's Hurricane Donna. However, when thousands of Haitian refugees sought refuge there in the 1980s, the area came to be known as Little Haiti.

In 1948, **Elizabeth Landsberg Virrick** began a campaign to improve living conditions in the Bahamian section of Coconut Grove, much of which still lacked indoor plumbing. With the aid of **Father Theodore Gibson**, they created the Citizens' Committee for Slum Clearance which was largely responsible for getting a City of Miami Ordinance passed that required each residential unit in the area be equipped with both a flush toilet and a sink, thus eliminating 482 public privies in The Grove.

Rev. Theodore Gibson

Elizabeth Virrick also founded "Coconut Grove Cares," a community center for ex-offenders and disadvantaged youths. She died in 1990 at the age of 93.

Elizabeth Landsburg Virrick

Government-supported desegregation throughout the nation escalated in the 1950s and '60s, with laws such as the (Dr. John O.) Brown Decision outlawing segregated schools in 1954. Fortunately, with **Robert King High** as Mayor of Miami and **Thomas LeRoy Collins** as Governor, this desegregation process was more easily accomplished in Florida than in many other southern states.

**Robert King High
on the Campaign Trail**

By January 7, 1970, all teachers, staff, administrators and schools were required to be integrated.

Thomas LeRoy Collins

Robert King High appointed John Culmer to Miami's first Committee for Peaceful Integration.

Throughout the decades some of black entertainment's greatest stars have called Miami their home, including the legendary **Billie Holiday, Ella Fitzgerald, Count Basie, Cab Calloway** and **Nat King Cole.** Actors **Ben Vereen** and **Sidney Poitier** are both home-grown Miami superstars with sand in their shoes.

Not allowed to live on the Island or stay in the local Miami Beach hotels in the early years, black entertainers had to live in Miami's Overtown area, which bussled with after-hours jazz clubs and honky-tonks.

Ella Fitzgerald

Billie Holiday

Nat "King" Cole

Sidney Poitier

"If you want to make beautiful music, you must play the black and white notes together."
- Richard Milhous Nixon

Reach for the Stars

"Houston, we have a problem." These were the chilling words spoken by astronaut **Jim Lovell** from the Apollo 13 space shuttle when an oxygen leak forced him and fellow astronauts **Fred Haise** and **Jack Swigert** to abandon ship and seek refuge in their ill-equipped lunar module.

At Mission Control, the man originally slotted to be the command module pilot of the mission, Miami Edison High School graduate and former Navy pilot **Ken Mattingly** spearheaded the ground crew's efforts to save the astronauts in a frantic race against time.

(Swigert replaced Mattingly just 72 hours prior to launch when Mattingly was exposed to German measles.)

Ken Mattingly

 Ken Mattingly finally made it into space in 1972, aboard Apollo 16 as pilot of the command module.

Frank Borman

It was fortunate that Lovell was aboard, as he had previous experience modifying the systems on another flight, Apollo 8 in 1968, our nation's first manned lunar orbital mission, with fellow astronauts **Bill Anders** and mission commander **Frank Borman**. On that flight, the first to have humans leave the Earth's gravitational influence, Lovell inadvertently got the computer "all fouled up" resulting in losing their guidance system, and Lovell had to realign the gyros manually. On "13," he had to perform this task deliberately.

Pinpoint accuracy was required to set the module's trajectory or risk shooting past the Earth thousands of miles off course into orbital oblivion. The astronauts had to rely on primitive celestial navigation techniques to set their course, but with Lovell's modifications and the grace of God, the lunar module, designed to last 45 hours and support two people (and certainly never designed to re-enter the Earth's atmosphere) miraculously sustained all three astronauts for a grueling 90 hours and successfully splashed down in the South Pacific on April 17, 1970, six days after launch.

The Miami connection? **Frank Borman**, commander of the Apollo 8 mission, as well as the Gemini 7 Space Orbital Rendezvous with Gemini 6 in 1965, became the CEO of Eastern Airlines in 1976, causing the airline to move their corporate headquarters from New York to Miami. Under his leadership, Eastern originated several innovative programs, including employee profit sharing and tying wages to company profitability, resulting in the four most profitable years in the airline's history.

In 1983, deregulation and a recalcitrant union forced Eastern to abandon these programs which led to the sale of the airline to Texas Air Corporation. Colonel Borman retired from Eastern Airlines in June of 1986.

"That's one small step for man, one giant leap for mankind."
   - Neil Armstrong on the first moonwalk – July 20, 1969

*In 1968, Apollo 8's **Frank Borman**, **Bill Anders** and **Jim Lovell** were named Time Magazine's Men of the Year.*

Honorable Mentions

"You can design and create, and build the most wonderful place in the world. But it takes people to make the dream a reality."

Walt Disney spoke those words and, like his Magic Kingdom, the Magic City gets its sparkle from the people who come through its gates.

Some of those people deserve special note, not for what they've achieved for themselves, but for what they've done for others – and for Miami.

Walt Disney

The teachers.

"The mediocre teacher tells. The good teacher explains. The superior teacher demonstrates. The great teacher inspires."

Ada Merritt was a teacher in Miami's first one-room school located in Lemon City at the turn of the century. She later taught in Miami and was honored by having Miami's first junior high school named for her.

Inspirational teacher, **Sister Gerald Barry** arrived in the United States in 1901 from County Clare, Ireland, and founded Miami's Barry University in 1940, as well as five other colleges and many other schools.

Another teacher, beloved author, **Dr. Thelma Peters**, lived in Miami Shores and taught at Miami Edison High School for 27 years.

 *Walt Disney negotiated with Mayor **Robert King High** to bring Disney World to Miami before he decided to build in Orlando.*

The ecologists.

"The only thing you take with you is what you leave behind," and two of Miami's newspaper editors left behind beautiful parks dedicated to preserving Miami's ecology and its history: **John D. Pennekamp,** who was editor of the *Miami Herald* during World War II, sponsored the formation of the *Everglades National Park* as well as the *Pennekamp Underwater State Park* in the Keys dedicated to preserving Florida's last natural reef; and

John D. Pennekamp

William C. "Bill" Baggs, late editor of the *Miami News,* whose namesake *Bill Baggs Cape Florida State Park* on Key Biscayne was built to preserve Florida's oldest landmark, the Cape Florida Lighthouse built in 1825.

William C. "Bill' Baggs

The philanthropists.

"Money is like manure. You have to spread it around or it smells."

Of those whose legacy to Miami came in the form of dollars, honorable mentions go to Miami banker and close friend of ex-President **Richard Nixon, Charles G. "Bebe" Rebozo,** who left $10 million to the Boys and Girls Club of Miami; and

Mitchell "Micky" Wolfson, Jr., who donated his entire 100,000 piece private collection of European and American decorative, design and advertising artifacts, valued at more than $75 million, to Wolfsonian-Florida International University; one of the largest philanthropic gifts ever to be contributed to a public university.

Mitchell "Micky" Wolfson, Jr.

 *Richard Nixon's Winter Whitehouse from 1969 to 1974 was on Key Biscayne, the area having been introduced to him by **Bebe Rebozo,** who was one of the owners of Fisher Island in the 1950s.*

Another South Florida benefactor, NY Yankees Hall of Famer, **Joe DiMaggio,** aka "The Yankee Clipper," retired to Hollywood, Florida shortly after his ill-fated 9-month marriage to the legendary **Marilyn Monroe.**

DiMaggio, the familiar "Mr. Coffee" spokesman in his later years, established the Joe DiMaggio Children's Hospital in Hollywood, part of the Memorial Healthcare System. Honored for its emergency care and nursing staff as well as its pediatric healthcare services, Joe DiMaggio Children's Hospital has one of the largest, most diverse groups of pediatric specialists in the region and is one of the premier providers of pediatric healthcare services in the country.

Joe DiMaggio and Marilyn Monroe

 Joe DiMaggio was a member of the LaGorce Country Club and could often be seen in the club's lounge, reminiscing about days gone by with other members and friends.

John Walsh

"Our children change us...whether they live or not."

No one was more touched by these poignant words than Florida's greatest advocate for victims' rights and missing children, **John Walsh,** host of "Americas Most Wanted," our nation's highest rated crime-fighting television show.

In 1981, while living in Florida and running a small travel and hotel consulting business in Bal Harbour, the Walsh's 6-year-old son, **Adam,** was kidnapped and later found murdered. Although the prime suspect in the murder was never charged (later dying in prison on unrelated charges), John and his wife, **Reve,** began a tireless campaign to help other missing and exploited children. This led to the passage of the "Missing Children Act" of 1982, and the "Missing Children's Assistance Act" of 1984, as well as the formation of the National Center for Missing and Exploited Children.

Author of several books and movies on the topic, in 1996, **John Walsh** was named by CBS as one of the "100 Americans Who Changed History."

"Some people are born great, some achieve greatness, and some have greatness thrust upon them."

Elian Gonzalez, coined *"El Niño Milagro," "the miracle child,"* became a defining part of Miami's future on Thanksgiving Day 1999, when a fisherman plucked him from the sea like Moses from the Nile.

With his mother dead from the treacherous voyage, 6-year-old Elian was taken to live with his great-uncle **Lazaro Gonzalez** and his family. An unwitting political pawn, Elian became the focus of worldwide attention when his father, **Juan Miguel Gonzalez,** still in Cuba, demanded Elian be returned to him.

"These were times that tried men's souls" and, when the U.S. Immigration and Naturalization Service (INS) determined that the father, **Mr. Juan Gonzalez,** had the sole legal authority to speak on behalf of his son, the city exploded.

After several attempts at negotiations, the world watched in horror as federal agents brandishing machine guns burst into the home of **Lazaro Gonzalez** in a surprise raid during the early pre-dawn hours of Easter Sunday 2000; the terrifying action forever caught on film by photographer **Alan Diaz,** who would win a Pulitzer Prize for the photo in 1991.

Taken to his father who then returned with the boy to Cuba, Elian's Miami relatives have not heard from him since. However, the rights of a father versus the right of every man to be free and to search for that freedom on American soil, has forever changed the politics of Miami and tarnished America's 50 stars in the eyes of the world.

The "Miami News and Metropolis" building (600 Biscayne Blvd.) became a meeting ground for Cuban exiles and came to be known as the "Freedom Tower." It is a symbol to all who would risk everything for freedom.

Wilson Mizner once said, *"The first hundred years are the hardest."* Miami celebrated its first hundred years in 1996. History may prove that Miami's most influential person may not yet be known to the world.

Maybe the next person who gets sand in his shoes is...you!

Elian Gonzalez Reunited With His Father

"The future belongs to those who believe in the beauty of their dreams."
- Eleanor Roosevelt

INDEX

Many sources were used as reference material for the contents of this book, including but not limited to, the thousands of websites available on the world-wide-web. Also utilized were interviews with long-time Miami residents, the teachings of Paul S. George, Ph.D. of Miami-Dade Community College and the wealth of information available at the Historical Association of Southern Florida.

Books & Printed Materials

"Memories of Old Miami"
By Hoyt Frazure as told to Nixon Smiley
Reprinted from a series of articles first appearing in Sunday Magazine of The Miami Herald

"Miami, The Way We Were"
By Howard Kleinberg, Editor of The Miami News
Miami Daily News 1985 – Printed by Vanderbilt Printing, Inc.

"Miami: The Magic City"
By Arva Moore Parks
Continental Heritage Press, Inc. 1981

"The Life and Times of Miami Beach"
By Ann Armbruster
Alfred A. Knopf, New York 1995

"Miami Beach, A History"
By Howard Kleinberg
Centennial Press 1994

"Florida Portrait. A Pictorial History of Florida"
By Jerrell Shofner
Pineapple Press, Inc. 1990

"A Journey Through Time. A Pictorial History of South Dade"
By Paul S. George
The Donning Company Publishers 1995

"Miami 1909 with Excerpts from Fannie Clemons' Diary"
By Thelma Peters
Banyan Books 1984

"Greater Miami and the Beaches Cultural Guide"
Greater Miami Convention and Visitors Bureau 2000

"All Fall Down. One Man Against the Waterfront Mob" by Donald Goddard
Published by TIMES BOOKS, a division of Quadrangle/The New York Times Book Co., Inc.
1980

"The Making of Miami Beach: 1933-1942. The Architecture of Lawrence Murray Dixon"
By Jean-Francois Lejeune and Allan T. Shulman
Published by Rizzoli International Publications, Inc.
Bass Museum of Art, Miami Beach, Florida 2000

"The Marshall Fields. A Study in Wealth"
By John Tebbel
E.P Dutton & Co., Inc., New York 1947

"The Dr. George Walking Tour of East Little Havana"
By Paul S. George, Ph.D.
The Historical Association of Southern Florida 1991

"Miami, U.S.A."
By Helen Muir
Hurricane House Publishers, Inc. 1953

"Miami Poppycock. The First 100 Years Centennial Issue"
By Ralph Bodek
Hallmark Press 1994

"Biscayne Country 1870-1926"
By Thelma Peters
Banyan Books, Inc. 1981

"In and Around South Miami 1776-1976. A Kaleidescope of the Past & Present"
By City of South Miami, South Miami Area Chamber of Commerce 1976

"Miami, The American Crossroad. A Centennial Journey 1896 – 1996"
By Arva Moore Parks and Gregory W. Bush with Laura Pincus
Simon & Schuster Custom Publishing 1996

"Julia's Daughters: Women in Dade's History"
A Research Project of Herstory of Florida, Inc.
Narrative by Marie Anderson
Herstory of Florida, Inc. 1980

"In the Company of Women."
Inspirational Portraits of Dade County Award Winners
The First Six Years 1989 – 1994

"The Commodore's Story. The Early Days on Biscayne Bay"
By Ralph Middleton Munroe and Vincent Gilpin - 1930
Historical Association of South Florida with support from the Knight Foundation 1990

"Touched by the Sun" The Florida Chronicles Volume 3
By Stuart B. McIver
Pineapple Press, Inc. 2001

"Tough Jews. Fathers, Sons, and Gangster Dreams"
By Rich Cohen
Simon & Schuster New York 1998

"Miami: Gateway to the Americas"
Edited by Miguel Gonzalez-Pando
Copperfield Publications, Inc. 1997

"Last Train to Paradise"
By Les Standiford
Crown Publishers, New York 2002

"Yesterday's Miami"
By Nixon Smiley with photographs by Richard B. Hoit and others
E. A. Seemann Publishing, Inc., Miami, Florida 1973

"Glimpses of South Florida History"
By Stuart McIver
Florida Flair Books, Miami, Florida 1988

"Old Miami Beach. A Case Study in Historic Preservation"
By H. Michael Raley, Linda G. Polansky and Aristides J. Millas
Miami Design Preservation League 1994

"Favorite Places Florida"
By Carole Chester
Multimedia Books Limited 1995

"Miami Memoirs"
By John Sewell / A New Pictorial Edition by Arva Moore Parks
Arva Moore Parks & Co., Miami, Florida 1987

"Dreamers, Schemers and Scalawags. The Florida Chronicles Volume I"
By Stuart B. McIver
Edwards Brothers, Lillington, NC 1994

"Florida Fun Facts"
By Eliot Kleinberg
Pineapple Press, Sarasota, Florida 1995

"Pop Culture"
By James P. Goss
Pineapple Press, Sarasota, Florida 2000

"Weird Florida"
By Eliot Kleinberg
Longstreet, Atlanta, Georgia 1997

"They All Called It Tropical"
By Charles M. Brookfield and Oliver Griswold
Historical Association of Southern Florida, Miami, Florida 1985

"Florida's Past. People & Events That Shaped the State. Volume 1"
By Gene M. Burnett
Pineapple Press, Sarasota, Florida 1986

"Florida's Past. People & Events That Shaped the State. Volume 2"
By Gene M. Burnett
Pineapple Press, Sarasota, Florida 1988

"Florida's Past. People & Events That Shaped the State. Volume 3"
By Gene M. Burnett
Pineapple Press, Sarasota, Florida 1991

"From Wilderness to Metropolis."
The History and Architecture of Dade County (1825 – 1940)
Metropolitan Dade County Office of Community and Economic Development
Historic Preservation Division
Franklin Press, Inc.

"Miami: The Sophisticated Tropics"
By Morton Beebe
Chronicle Books, San Francisco 1991

Historical Association of Southern Florida
Florida Photographic Collection
Ralph Munroe Collection, Historical Association of Southern Florida
Romer Collection, Miami-Dade Public Library

Plus hundreds of sites on the world-wide-web.

About The Author

Sandy Thorpe

Sandy moved to Miami from Chicago in 1988, and began working for Marty Taplin in 1996.

A master storyteller, Marty regaled her with tales of a different Miami, "his Miami," as he experienced it as a young child during World War II, when he watched in awe as troops marched down Collins Avenue, and then in later years, as he saw South Beach bloom, the building boom and the transformation of Miami from a resort town into an international city.

Intrigued, Sandy became a student of history at Miami-Dade Community College and developed a deep appreciation for Miami -- and for the people who put the "magic" in the "Magic City."

An admitted "Trekkie," Sandy's first passion is *Star Trek*© and she has traveled all over the world on her "never ending mission to seek out new life and new civilizations" in the Star Trek© Universe.

She is also an accomplished artist and her screen credits include brief appearances in both *Trekkies* - and *Trekkies 2!*